Out of Chaos

A New Vision
For Schools
and Communities

**The real issue is that our public education system
is obsolete and must be reinvented.**

Matt W. Beck, M.Ed.

For Passion Publishing Company
Bellingham, Washington U.S.A.

FOR-PASSION
PUBLISHING

Published by For Passion Publishing Company, LLC
Dr. Daniel Levine
P.O. Box 28312
Bellingham WA   U.S.A. 98228

ForPassionPublishing@gmail.com

www.ForPassionPublishing.com

First Edition.

ISBN 978-1530164868

Printed in the United States of America.

"We have a new problem in American public schools, and most people have no real idea how it will be solved or even the dimensions of the difficulty: we must make sure that ALL students have both the skills and values they need for work and citizenship in a rapidly changing world."

Tony Wagner, Author, Making the Grade: Reinventing America's Schools.

This Book's Cover

Play the Game!

The dart board on the front cover suggests a game, or a tool, you can use to rate your child's school. In the book is an activity which will help you understand the current capacity of your child's school with preparing your child for a happy and healthy life as an adult who will be living into his or her 80s. Please read the description and instructions below!

The Reason for the Cover Image

The cover shows a dart board to communicate that the public schools are aiming at the wrong target, and as a metaphor to illustrate the correct target as described in this book. In the activity presented later in this book, the total points available add up to 100:

> 1. The center has three areas, each worth 10 points for a total of 30.
> 2. The second circle has two areas, each worth 8 points for a total of 16.
> 3. The third circle has eight areas, each worth 6 points for a total of 48.
> 4. The outer circle has 4 areas, each worth 1 or 2 points for a total of 4.

Instructions on How to Play the Game

As you read this book, you will learn what the different segments represent and why they have been allocated their various point values.

At the end of the book is a measuring device, called a rubric, which you can use for assessing how well-prepared your child will be to enjoy his or her life as a healthy adult.

How well will your child's school score?

Read this book and then use the rubric at the back!

Building Healthy Children

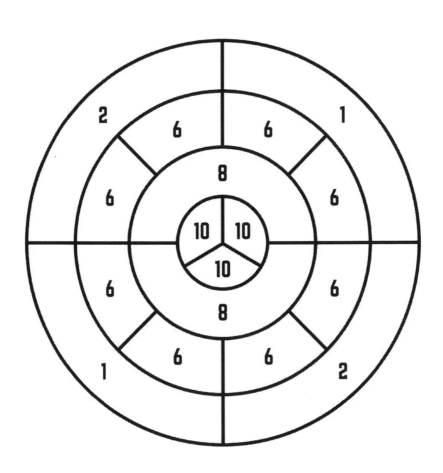

Key to the Dartboard Diagram
(100 points possible)

Child's Needs:
- Family and Extended Family: 10 points
- Good Role Models: 10 points
- Hobbies and Interests: 10 points

Essential Traits to Develop, Tier 1:
- Kindness and Compassion: 8 points
- How to Save Money: 8 points

Essential Traits to Develop, Tier 2:
- Leadership: 6 points
- Responsibility: 6 points
- Teamwork: 6 points
- Dedicated Work Ethics: 6 points
- Good Eating Habits: 6 points
- Good Problem Solving Strategies and Good Choices: 6 points
- Parenting Skills: 6 points
- Healthy Relationships: 6 points

Academics, Outer Ring:
- Reading: 2 points
- Math: 2 points
- Writing: 1 points
- History: 1 point

A score of 80 points or better gives your child the best chance for life-long success and happiness. Go to the scoring rubrics on page 91 and give your child's school a grade!

Can You Answer These 10 Questions?

These questions are to help you start thinking about education and how our public school system might be reinvented. Please take a moment with each question and see if they begin to stimulate your thinking.

1. Is our current public school system functioning well? If so, what do you like most? If you think the schools should be improved, what would you want changed the most?

2. Should our schools focus primarily on teaching the current curriculum?

3. Do you believe that the public school system provides a child's basic needs for a productive, satisfying adult life?

4. What do you think is the most important ability a child should have when he or she graduates from the public schools?

5. When you think of a healthy person, what attributes do they have?

6. Do you think the public school system is sufficiently funded, or should it have a larger budget?

7. Do you believe most parents can raise their children to become healthy adults?

8. Do children have untapped potential that the public schools are unable to develop?

9. Is having good character more important than solving math equations?

10. Are you willing to support significant public education changes?

More Praise for
Out of Chaos
A New Vision for Schools
and Communities

"If you are seeking the continued unraveling of our social fabric and admire the inability of our current school system to improve student learning, don't read this book." Dr. Betty Willet, retired public school superintendent, Sonoma County, CA.

"Everyone who has a child in the public school system should put this book in the hands of their district's school board members. The problem with public education today is the state education leaders who are not education leaders at all." Dr. Donna Thomson, former school board member, Virginia Beach City Public Schools.

"Mr. Beck has put his finger precisely on the problem. Our public schools are filled with dedicated people who want to help children but are frustrated by a task that always places the cart before the horse." Dr. Mark Reitan, teacher trainer, Santa Rosa Junior College.

"It's time for a big change. My hope is there will be a school district courageous enough to try these changes. My family and I will move there today." Rebecca Simmons, parent.

"I wish I wasn't wasting my time in school." Larissa V., sixth grade student.

"We are shut up in schools...for ten or fifteen years, and come out at last with a bag of wind, a memory of words, and do not know a thing."

Ralph Waldo Emerson, philosopher.

Disclaimer

This book is presented solely for educational purposes and is not intended to represent or be used as an exhaustive resource for any purpose. The information contained in this book represents only the viewpoints of the individual author.

The author, editors and For Passion Publishing Company emphasize this material is not offered as being complete professional advice. It is highly recommended you contact the author before making any decisions regarding your educational program.

Best efforts have underscored the writing of this book, but the author, editors, and publisher make no representations or warranties of any kind and assume no liabilities of any kind with respect to the accuracy or completeness of the contents, and specifically disclaim any implied warranties of use for any particular purpose.

Neither the author, editors, nor For Passion Publishing Company shall be held liable or responsible to any person or entity with respect to any loss or incidental or consequential damages caused, or alleged to have been caused, directly or indirectly, by the information contained in this book, or disruption caused by errors or omissions, whether such errors or omissions result from negligence, accident, or any other cause.

Any likeness to actual persons, either living or dead, other than those represented by the author as persons known to him, is completely coincidental.

Dedication

This book is dedicated to my parents, Robert and Bonna Beck, my siblings and their spouses, Tami/Greg Merit, Bret/Debbie Beck, Jodi Ruzicka, and Rita/Johnny Brandt, and my children, Brandon, Ashley, Krista, and their families.

This book is also dedicated to all the parents, teachers, and administrators who are doing their best every day under conflicting circumstances to help children and youth grow into their full capacity as kind, compassionate and loving people.

Equally, this book is dedicated to the thousands of children I have had the privilege of teaching and coaching. You taught me everything.

About the Author
Matt W. Beck, M. Ed.

Matt W. Beck has dedicated his life to teaching children and young adults the values of good character, kindness, compassion, and service to others in his work as a teacher and coach during his 33 years as a professional educator.

A lifetime advocate for children, Mr. Beck has received several awards recognizing him for his service to the children and parents of his community, and his students have won recognition in community events. Mr. Beck has created and implemented several successful programs at his schools, including the Real Hero Mentoring Program which elevated relationships between children, the school, and the community.

Mr. Beck has also published over 20 instructional books, resulting in one elementary school achieving the highest state assessment scores in science.

Matt has a Masters Degree in Education from the University of

Portland, is a certified school administrator, and outside of school he founded or cofounded four nonprofit organizations to support children and families. He cofounded an educational publishing company to help students develop problem solving, critical thinking skills and the love of learning while improving standardized test scores in math and science. Matt was the cofounder of a Boys and Girls Club for which he later served as President, and was subsequently recognized as the Coach of the Year.

Matt lives in northwest Washington, close to the Canadian border where he and his brother, Dr. Bret Beck, a scientist at Lawrence Livermore National Laboratory, grew up on a working farm. Matt has raised three wonderful children; his son, Brandon, recently earned a Master's Degree in Business from Vanderbilt University, scored in the top 1% on the GMAT exam and is currently employed with the Microsoft Corporation. Matt's two daughters, Ashley and Krista, both graduated from four year colleges with high grades, but most importantly they are kind, compassionate and healthy adults who are contributing to a better community and a better future for younger generations.

Acknowledgements

I wish to personally thank the following individuals who without their contributions and support this book would not have been written:

My immediate and extended family who are truly too many to mention, which has made me aware of how critically important a life-long support system of family and friends is to the health of all.

My co-workers of administrators, teachers, and aides who have supported my efforts to best serve the students we shared and provided me with the love and encouragement I needed.

The following educational leaders around the country with whom I have had the pleasure of working in my extensive activities outside my school district: Terry Pickeral, board member, Collaborative for Academic, Social and Emotional Learning (CASEL); Dr. Betsy Rogers, National Teacher of the Year; Veronique Paquette, the Washington State Teacher of the Year; Jane Robertson, Arizona Teacher of the Year; and Betty Hopkins, Mississippi Teacher of the Year.

Dr. Daniel Levine, retired public school superintendent ; Dr. Jeffrey Piontek, science education consultant for Texas Education Agency, New York City Department of Education, and Hawaii Department of Education; Dr. Richard Vineyard, Assistant Director of Curriculum, Nevada Department of Education; Deborah Boros, National President of the Society of Elementary Presidential Awardees; and Michelle Boyd, Recipient, Presidential

Award for Excellence in Mathematics and Science Teaching.

Dr. Michael Naylor, Associate Professor of Mathematics, Western Washington University; Mary Bennett Moore, Stewart "Andy" Anderson, Georgi Delgadillo, and Brian Teppner, science authors and members of the Science Assessment Leadership Team, Olympia, WA; Roxann Rose-Duckworth, Disney American Teacher; and Dan Persse, finalist, National Teacher of the Year, AAHPERD.

Nita Wright, 2015 Teacher of the Year Finalist; Tom Luehman, retired principal, King's High School, Seattle; Pam Pottle, principal, Bellingham School District; Dr. Donald Bauthues, retired public school superintendent; Mr. Bruce Taubenheim, retired principal; Mr. Jon Abbott, former school counselor; and Jim Lissner, exceptional fifth grade teacher, Meridian School District. You are all so genuinely dedicated to the well-being of all our children!

As I weathered the storm of life, it was these individuals who gave me support and hope that there really are genuine people dedicated to the betterment of all. You truly are my heroes and made it possible for me to write this book. Thank you!

Dr. Daniel Levine of For Passion Publishing for editing, coordinating all the aspects of the book, and publishing. It was a pleasure working with Daniel, who exemplifies the idea that professionalism and kindness are compatible behaviors.

I also appreciate the dedication of my publishing team for preparing this book: Anika Klix, associate editor; Zander Levine, assistant editor; and Hayden LeMaster for expert technical skills.

Foreword

I have the pleasure of writing the foreword for Matt's new book, and I am honored and grateful. I've known Matt for over a dozen years and I've worked closely with him on several educational projects over many of those years. We collaborated with publishing exceptional instructional materials that created an urgency in children to learn, and we also worked on a project to build character in children, yet not just in children but also in parents, teachers, coaches, adults of all ages, civic leaders, business people, celebrities...

That's the thing about Matt. He doesn't think big...he thinks huge. Wait a minute, maybe huge isn't large enough...try enormous. Better yet, capitalize it and stick an exclamation point on the end···Enormous! There, that's better. When Matt sets his mind and his heart to something, you can bet that it can change life on Earth.

And this is what Matt has done with this book, Out of Chaos. Matt is an original thinker with a clear vision of how things should be. He is a lifetime professional educator like I am...but he saw what I didn't, what none of us have. He was able to look at the same dysfunctional messy school system that every one of us sees, and his Vision penetrated the darkness and took all the pieces we know will work...we KNOW will work...and put each piece together with the others to bring you, and all of us, the crystallized version of a comprehensible, comprehensive, and realistic system that can change the public schools...and our self-destructing society...and create the possibilities for a humane future for our nation and, really, for all humankind.

That's the scale of this Vision, and that's the point of this book. No one is happy with our public school system. Nobody. So what are we going to do? Throw more money at it? No. Continue to make changes that have no significant effect? No. Train better teachers? No. Let the whole system implode? No. Explode? No. Continue harming our children with classes that make kids feel like they are harnessed to a horse-drawn single shovel plow? No.

NO!

Matt has a unique viewpoint of how to change our country's collapsing school system, and his ideas need to be implemented immediately. The ideas in this book are fresh and compelling, and I know...KNOW...they will work.

What concerns me most about our educational decision-makers is not that they may misunderstand the need and urgency for complete educational reinvention, but rather that their arrogance and ignorance will deliberately prevent every possibility for significant changes. I believe these so-called educational leaders (politicians, state and national administrators, philanthropists, consultants, and businessmen) have no understanding about the children and families they supposedly serve, and will only achieve minimal success with a minimal number of students...while the overwhelming majority of children and families continue to spiral out of control.

I have invested over 30 years in education...I've been a middle school and junior high school teacher, a principal, a superintendent...I have a doctorate in education...I've written and published high-quality instructional materials...and I've witnessed the lethargy, disappointment, misdirections, confusing state and federal half-measures, the lost resources both human and monetary, the angry parents, the well-intentioned but perplexed school board members...and worst of all, the children and youth who are being shortchanged on the promise of a good and healthy life in a caring community.

What happened? We lost our way. But Matt has a great compass and a great map. Read this book. Don't get caught in the weeds...go for The Big Picture. The thing I know about educators, even people in general, is that we (okay, not you..."they"...) look for things to pick at so they can say, "Oh! This won't work! And this won't either!" It's a small-minded person who does this.

But not you! You will see the wisdom behind these concepts, you will understand the value and practical application of these ideas, and you will get excited by the Enormous possibility! And you will give a copy of this book to your school board members and your child's principal, and bring it up for discussion at board meetings, and at the PTA, and with your child's teacher...

Matt and I will do what we can. Now we need you. Please join us.

Dr. Daniel Levine
Father of an amazing teenage son

You must realize what I have come to believe with all my heart:

Our children have immense potential.

All they need are the opportunities to reach their potential from the adults to whom they are entrusted for care.

HOWEVER, this opportunity will never occur unless the school system drastically changes from the focus of an academically capable person to building a healthy person and community in much the same way that an engineer would design a state-of-the-art plane, bridge, or skyscraper. Those who are in a position of leadership and power should be the best and most capable educators (engineers) for building healthy people and communities. UNFORTUNATELY, this is not the case and instead they are making decisions that are presenting false hope to the families entrusted in their care, and greatly adding to the downward spiral of a child's opportunity for a healthy and content adult life.

We all can basically agree on the needs for children and which essential traits are critical for a healthy adult life, YET we continue to watch people of influence make decisions that are completely off-target with preparing a child for adulthood. I believe most teachers go to work feeling frustrated every day because all we hear from the people in power is strong lip service about the needs and essential traits for children, but the darts continue to be thrown at assessments, teacher training and evaluation, school vouchers, state standards, higher expectations, and the No Child Left Behind Act. They continue to put the cart before the horse. This insanity needs to stop. IT WILL NEVER WORK! These people of influence are living a content life themselves, while steering their flock down a road of self-destruction.

On the front end we keep throwing billions of dollars into a broken educational system to support new ideas ONLY to make it more broken, which is causing present generations great harm and suffering.

On the backend we keep throwing billions of dollars into addiction rehabilitation, prison reform, and social welfare programs to take care of the people our educational system didn't properly prepare for a healthy adult life.

Contents

"I was compelled to read this entire book... You are suggesting core, substantive changes, which is what we need."

Michael Reist, Author, What Every Parent Should Know About School.

Part 1
The Current Situation

This is a book about how we can give our children lives worth living by changing our public school system from the bloated dysfunctional disaster it is today into a system that builds healthy people with productive and satisfying lives...a modern school system that teaches people how to live well and live a rewarding life with strong relationships, positive values, and self-contentment.

You can go to a bookstore and see shelves of books about school reform, but not a single one of them is like the book you are about to read. New ideas about education are rare, and this is a book that presents new ideas with a realistic overview for implementation so your children can have the life of your dreams for them.

When you have finished reading Part 1, you will:

- Realize that public schools are focused on the wrong outcomes.
- Discern that the current educational system is building the roof before the foundation.
- Recognize that the public school system does not provide a child's basic needs for a productive, satisfying life.
- Understand the concept of engineering as a way to think about school change.
- Be able to explain 14 influences that are destroying our country.

- Know we do not really have educational leaders, just educational managers.
- Possess introductory knowledge about the condensed history of our nation's school system.
- Acknowledge that most parents cannot raise their children to become healthy adults.
- Accept that our religious and community organizations are equally helpless.
- Be open to thinking about education in a completely new light.

I hope you find the new ideas you will read on the next pages interesting and compelling. Change is necessary and your involvement is necessary and valued.

Two Online Videos You Must Watch

Here are two exceptional videos you must watch because they are so important for your deeper understanding of public education today, and public education tomorrow. Watching both videos will take less than 30 minutes and worth every second.

1.   Please watch "Changing Education Paradigms." It has over 13,500,000 views, indicating the level of interest it has attracted. This video is about 11 minutes long and was created by Sir Ken Robinson, an author, speaker, and international advisor on education. To watch this video, go to YouTube and type in the link, or go to YouTube and enter these keywords: Changing Education Paradigms. https://www.youtube.com/watch?v=zDZFcDGpL4U [1]

2.   Please watch "Khan Academy: The future of education?" This 60 Minutes CBS News report has over 430,000 views and is 13 minutes long. You may have heard of the Khan Academy; it's quite popular and your children may already be participants. Bill Gates has said, "Khan is teacher to the world, giving us all a glimpse of the future of education." Salman Khan says, "We're trying to take passivity out of the classroom so the teacher has more flexibility." To watch this video, go to YouTube and type in the link, or go to YouTube and enter these keywords: Khan Academy The Future of Education. https://www.youtube.com/watch?v=zxJgPHM5NYI [2]

Note: All footnotes are identified in the back of this book.

"Change your thoughts and you change your world."

Norman Vincent Peale

Introduction

I firmly believe there is a tremendous need for our public school system. We need a system that gives each child the best chance for reaching his or her full potential. The current system is failing and our students are bored, unfulfilled, dropping out, and unable to achieve the learning goals mandated by state education personnel. Why is this happening? This huge failure is a result of the schools being focused on the completely wrong target. The schools believe their primary purpose is to improve academic outcomes in reading, math, and science, and I propose this is an absolutely incorrect priority.

Our nation's schools are not able to educate children and teenagers because schools are focused on academics, and in this book I will show why academics are the wrong target. I will also propose ways to improve the public school system so children and teenagers can enjoy a more productive and satisfying life.

As you read this book, please keep the following metaphor in mind. Our public school system is like an engineering company that has been contracted to construct a building. Without a proper foundation, the walls and roof will not hold. It is my belief that the current school system's foundation is poorly constructed, and I'll explain why.

Furthermore, this second, additional metaphor is appropriate. Imagine that the public schools are an ice cream cone holding large scoops of ice cream; adding more ice cream (money, programs, teachers, assessments...) will not help, but instead will create an even bigger mess! I'll also explain why this is so in this book.

> ## Why are our schools focused on the wrong target?

We need to make significant changes. Our schools will continue to be completely ineffective until they defocus from their current intention of creating an academically capable person and instead focus on creating a healthy person. This is a radical shift from the underlying assumptions of the current system, but I contend that we will see failure after failure until this shift occurs.

We need to look at creating a healthy person in much the same way that an engineer looks at building a building. An engineer would never allow an unsafe building to be constructed. In the same way "people-engineers" can build a healthy person. We need engineers who can fix the incredible problems we're facing now, and create an improved system that sets our children and youth on the right path for a healthy life. This book proposes a drastic change from what educational leaders/managers are doing and what a visionary engineer would do.

I am a teacher who has worked with our K – 12 population for over 30 years, and I have a broad range of valuable experiences both in and out of school that have helped me come to many insightful conclusions. I believe that as a whole, teachers, administrators and those who work with children and youth are highly dedicated to their work and want the best for students. I don't believe teachers are to blame; it is the system that has no chance of succeeding. In fact, within the current dysfunctional system, many good-hearted and well-intentioned people are actually overachieving in the academic outcomes, despite the odds working against them.

Most teachers are hard-working, and dedicated to following the path laid out for them by state officials. The teachers, principals, and superintendents are all doing what is being asked of them...but what they are being asked to do is inconsequential.

The current system does not provide the basic needs for a child to have the best chance for a kind, compassionate, competent, and productive experience as a member of society. Take a look around. Our society is struggling with welfare, a high dropout rate, uncontrolled debt, overcrowded prisons, etc. It's as though our schools are modeled after the foster care program with children moving from homeroom to homeroom throughout their public school experience, and regularly becoming detached from the people who care about them and who could otherwise become a lifelong support person. We are installing metal detectors, security guards, police officers, and more vice principals to deal with the majority of students who don't fit into the box. Instead of providing our children with a positive role model during the trying middle and high school years, we allow the media to direct our children's behavior.

Our society can NEVER improve as it is now.

The change we need can never come from our current political and social systems. Many people of influence in our communities, states, nation, and the world are book-smart but completely deficient in the qualities that heal and unite.

Our teachers, who should be building a healthy nation, are off-target from their true purpose, which is instilling positive life-long qualities in children during their formative years.

Schools and teachers are capable of making the significant changes we need when we shift their focus to building healthy children.

Competitive after-school sports is another example of how we are failing our children; so is the lack of an effective school program that exposes children to a multitude of interests and activities that only a privileged few are able to enjoy.

Another concern is that our schools are littered with employees (principals, secretaries, teachers, and others) who are emotionally challenged, and work against the best interests of the child and the community. These people are bullies, and they would be more useful serving on the front lines in the Middle East fighting terrorism. There is absolutely no place for bullies in a system that is building a healthy child.

• When you read this book, you'll understand why the current public school system is broken and failing.

• When you read this book, you will see the value of focusing on building healthy children instead of educated children.

• When you read this book, you'll wonder why we don't look at building healthy children the same way we build buildings, airplanes, bridges, etc.

> "This has been the most difficult task I have had to face as a teacher···working within a system while seeing its problems and the damage it does to individuals." -Michael Reist, author of "What Every Parent Should Know About School".

• When you read this book, you'll wonder why we have teachers and managers who are pounding assessment preparation into our children.

• When you read this book, you will discover that no more money needs to be dumped into education.

• When you read this book, you'll learn why we have the current educational structure, and specific ways to implement a new design that will change your community and give your children the prospects for enjoying a happy, healthy, and prosperous life.

The focus of the public school system should be building a healthy person.

The Purpose of This Book

This is a unique book. Its intention is to shatter your assumptions about education, schools, and public schools in particular. This book also proposes the premise for a new structure for our nation's communities based on kindness, compassion, an individual's true self-worth, and a radical vision of how we must adjust ourselves, our thinking, our behavior and our expectations to co-create a more healthy, productive, meaningful and sustainable life in the 21st Century.

Our country is in a downward spiral...and it appears there is no end in sight. Almost every adult feels the challenges personally and is concerned about the future for our youth. Many people feel education is the answer. It has frequently been the case that people in positions of influence (politicians, teacher organizations, state school officers) believe that dumping more money into education, hiring better teachers, and improving test scores is the answer to fixing the woes of society.

> Educational leaders and politicians have taken us backward as they continually try to fit a round peg into a square hole. It's time this stopped.

Over the past 20 years and more, this fictitious solution has only been a huge distraction and has never come close to the root of the problem nor made any progress toward fixing it. Like the ice cream cone metaphor, only a bigger mess was created. However, what I am about to share with you will show you a different perspective on how we got here and a truly viable means for fixing it. I have shared my thoughts and beliefs with hundreds of people and NOT ONE person has ever disagreed with the substance and concrete ideas I've proposed to change the madness that is causing tremendous harm to our community's youth and their chance for a happy, meaningful and healthy life.

After you read this book, please don't remain idle. There will be suggestions later in this book about how you can take action and participate locally and globally with making the extremely important changes necessary for our children's future and the future of our nation. Your involvement is crucial for reversing this very harmful downward spiral as we continue to witness a large percentage of young children, like their parents, not reaching a minimal achievement of their life's dreams.

The book you are holding is deliberately a rather thin book, i.e., it was not designed to be a giant discourse on the ills of education and society. The bookshelves are already heavy with ponderous tomes crammed with educated language that quickly disenfranchise the reader with their bulk. Instead, the content of this book is meant to be direct and simplistic so its points can be clearly understood and quickly assimilated.

Our primary goal as engineers:
We want to build a healthy person.

This book is meant to engage you with its concepts and plausibility, providing you with an introduction to the possibilities of co-creating a new educational system that will truly reward every child, relieve teachers of their currently undue burdens, restructure the schools to be more effective and efficient systems of delivery without increased expenditures, engage parents to the extent of their means and welcome them as participants like never before, and change our communities from their current state of fractured and inconsistent service into a cohesive, highly functional, inclusive and responsive network of neighbors living together for the common good of every individual.

The content you are about to read is organized into six parts:

Part 1:	The Current Situation
Part 2:	What Children Really Need
Part 3:	Restructuring the Schools
Part 4:	Making Change a Reality
Part 5:	The Scoring Rubric: How Well Does Your School Score?
Part 6:	What You Can Do Now
Part 7:	Addenda: More Online Videos; The Real Hero Mentor Program; The Puzzlewise Program; Footnotes

The current situation may be redundant to the continual discord one already hears in the news or witnesses in personal life. Still, there is value in seeing the situation in a new light because this perspective is imperative to revealing the new vision. Yes, our schools are troubled. Yes, our communities are not as strong and capable as we would like. Yes, our nation is facing a variety of hazards, both internally and globally. However, though this is the case, by viewing these circumstances through a different lens, as will be proposed in the first section, the difficulties we now face will clarify and augment the value of the proposed solution.

As for the solution itself, some may be immediately clear, and some will need to be co-created. The nature of our democracy invites participation and decision-making, and for a system to be effective for all its members, everyone must be engaged with its development.

The main point of this introduction is to begin with the acknowledgment that our schools and our society are failing our children, and some action must be taken other than dumping more money into a broken system during our children's formative years only to make it more broken. This wasteful tragedy is compounded by dumping even more money into programs during our children's adult years to rehabilitate drug or alcohol addiction, pay for prisons, and pay for social programs that provide food, medical care, housing, etc...ALL because we wrongly chose to aim at academic outcomes during the critical formative years. We must take action now to reverse the trend and the damage, and create the opportunity for a healthy life for everyone.

This book describes the situation and presents a realistic solution to save, restore, and advance America and the lives of our children.

"When I went to school, they asked me what I
wanted to be when I grew up. I wrote down "HAPPY".

They told me I did not understand the assignment
and I told them they did not understand LIFE."

John Lennon

The Role of Engineers
in Building a Healthy Child

One of the most important concepts you must understand about working with children is the idea of ENGINEERS.

Engineers have developed amazing electrical, mechanical, computer, and architectural systems. They have made it possible for people to work and live on the 50th floor of giant buildings that are structurally sound and even safe during large earthquakes. Engineers have made great advances that have enhanced the quality of our lives. They study a task and then apply their education and experience to complete the task.

We have seen tremendous advances in so many areas of our life...in medicine, telecommunications, air travel...yet why haven't we seen the same advances in education? Is it because we haven't looked at education in the same way? Our schools have made almost no changes at all in the last 100 years. You've heard the joke that if Rip van Winkle had just awakened, he would see no difference in the schools. Why is this so? Why have we made great improvements in almost every aspect of our lives except education? Why are there no education engineers?

What should schools teach? Why is the curriculum in our schools focused on academics, rather than more essential areas? Are academics what we really value the most?

As adults interested in child development, whether you are a parent or an educator, are we merely looking to improve our children's ability to add 2 + 2, read Jack and Jill, or spell C-A-T?

Are these the educational outcomes we most desire? It would seem so.

Yet these are the outcomes of an academic design, not a design intended to produce healthy people. A healthy person has a distinctly different set of characteristics. Discussed in greater detail later, the important aspects of a healthy person include being kind and compassionate, financially responsible, volunteering in the community, eating a wholesome diet, learning how to create and maintain healthy relationships, etc. Can we agree that the outcomes of a healthy person are more desirable than merely the outcomes of an educated person?

Schools spend over 30 classroom hours each week dedicated to improving academic areas and 10,000+ hours on every K-12 student only to discover that the children entrusted to their care end up deficient in reading and mathematics, scoring significantly lower than other countries. How can this be when we are spending more cash per child than any other country?

The answer is very clear...

The educational institution is aiming at the wrong target. Our legions of educators keep pouring billions of dollars into a system that has no hope...NO HOPE...of making any meaningful improvements.

THE WRONG TARGET!

Of course we haven't seen any improvements in educational outcomes! Our schools are trying to improve test scores by building from the top down! Because the foundation of the structure hasn't been properly built, the structure will always collapse. Though you will often hear administrators and teachers verbalize what they believe are the critical needs of children and how to address them, they are always off target. The needs of a healthy child are overlooked because educators are focused on constructing the building in the wrong sequence! Our educational leaders are not really leaders at all··· The word "leader" implies the gift of having an inspired vision. Instead, these people are managers and quality control experts for a system that is manufacturing damaged goods that are unwanted by dissatisfied captive customers.

Most of these individuals are well-intended, but when they get together, they become paralyzed with the same old ideas of spending more money, school vouchers, improving test scores, making class sizes smaller, teacher evaluation tools, and using merit pay to motivate teachers. None of these will work without first restructuring the broken system.

If these same educational experts and leaders managed an engineering firm, we would probably still be using logs to build bridges or flying in a two-seater airplane that's limited to only one mile. In other words, progress would be minimal or nonexistent. Actually, because education hasn't kept up with the changes in our society, we have truly gone backwards, resulting in tremendous pain and suffering.

Let's use the analogy of designing and constructing a sturdy two-story building with a penthouse on the second floor. An engineer knows that the most important part of this structure is its foundation. Without a strong base that can carry weight and weather storms, the first story and the penthouse simply will not survive. This is common sense, but as you will see, our experts have chosen to build the penthouse first. Billions of dollars every year are being poured into teacher development and improving test scores but it is all pointless and a terrible waste that will never achieve the desired results. You have repeatedly heard the bad news for the last several decades. This will not and cannot change.

"Only about 30% of the time spent in high school is used for learning. The rest of the time is unnecessarily wasted when teachers spend too much time helping slower learners, without giving the rest of the class anything to work on." Zander L., 4.0 high school student, now enrolled in an independent learning school.

The effect of all these billions of dollars and hundreds of thousands of hours of effort by teachers, children, and parents is that we have created a beautiful penthouse with all the bells and whistles seated upon a weak foundation and a flimsy first floor. This educational structure will never be strong and will endlessly continue to collapse. We need to stop pouring money into the system and stop supporting the politicians and educational managers who are only giving the public false hope about improving test scores and the pretended benefits they will provide. We also need to stop pointing fingers at the teachers, accusing them of being the problem.

The schools are focused on the wrong target, plain and simple.

When you stop to think about it, our nation has millions of people who are considered to be well-educated. We have bankers, Wall Street investment brokers, attorneys, doctors and nurses, administrators of all kinds, principals, superintendents, college professors, etc. They have undergraduate and graduate degrees in all areas of human knowledge and yet most of these adults are deficient in the essential parts of being a healthy person. Regarded in this light, their knowledge and service has actually contributed to the downward spiral our country is now experiencing. Their contribution to the greater good and to future generations dependent on the decisions they've made and are making today are highly detrimental. Because they are not healthy people themselves, they have co-created a nation that is now in severe trouble. Perhaps we would have been better off without their contribution.

So let's ask this question, a question that takes us off the beaten path and points us in a new direction: How would someone who is an expert with engineering a child improve the philosophy and methods currently in use in our dysfunctional school system?

If we hired an engineering firm to build a healthy person, it's highly unlikely that they would begin with the academic part first. Frankly, it would be ridiculous. As engineers, they would know to begin with the basic foundation of what a child needs. They would address the essential areas a child needs to develop, and then support and mature the elements that constitute a whole and healthy child. One of the last of the sequential tasks, not the first, would be helping a child prepare for earning a college degree or learning a technical trade that will help him or her become self-sufficient with furthering his or her goals, dreams and aspirations.

How do you build a healthy person?

Most educational leaders believe and would say they are building a healthy person, but an expert in building a healthy person, our educational engineer, would emphatically disagree. As it exists today, our educational system is completely ineffective and failing miserably. When you look closely at the current ability of the public school system for engineering healthy people, you can see that becoming a healthy person is an impossibility. We need to change the way we perform these essential tasks, and develop a new system for building healthy people.

The Current Horrifying Situation

The following has become too familiar over the last 30 or 50 years. Still, you may find yourself unwillingly fascinated by the damage that afflicts our country, our local communities, the lives of the people around us and, sadly, the lives of our own family. The scope of the situation cannot be minimized. The combination of these negative influences is dissolving our society, and is likely to result in the demise of our nation.

1. Poor School Results Because of the Wrong Target.

Every year billions of dollars are spent by our public school system···and the results continue to be minimal and dismal. Reading and math scores continually indicate that about half the student population is not assessing at their grade level. Though there are exceptions, the American public knows that millions of students are not meeting reasonable standards.

At regular intervals, new national or state mandates are created to re-energize the failing system so every child can become educationally successful. You've heard about the No Child Left Behind Act of 2001, which replaced the 1965 Elementary and Secondary Education Act. The No Child Left Behind Act has now been replaced by the Every Student Succeeds Act of 2015.

"Every few years, along comes a new idea to save American schools, be it enforcing standards, opening charter schools, providing vouchers for private education, or paying teachers based on their performance. All this activity has generated progress in some areas, but it has not led to widespread improvement. U.S. schools still languish in the middle of international rankings, behind the schools of such countries as Estonia and Slovenia."

"Why American Education Fails," Jal Mehta.

Teachers have been exposed to an endless array of learning theories including behaviorism, cognitivism, constructivism, and now the newest, connectivism. New methodology and practices to help students learn have been paraded before weary faculties who are tired of the pageantry and now daydream about early retirement.

2. Excessive Addictions.

We live in an addicted society. Unless you are an alcoholic or know one, it would never occur to you how many of your neighbors are looking forward to an end-of-the-day drink, or an end-of-the-day bottle. Many people are addicted to alcohol and don't realize it.

Consider the underground use of marijuana. Several states have approved its recreational use, and more states will soon do so. Cocaine, of course, is available with the right connections. Now there is an epidemic of heroin use because people have become addicted to pain medications controlled by the medical and pharmacy industries.

> "In 2010 almost 1 in 20 adolescents and adults –
> 12 million people – used prescription pain medication
> when it was not prescribed for them or only for the
> feeling it caused. While many believe these drugs are
> not dangerous because they can be prescribed by a
> doctor, abuse often leads to dependence. And
> eventually, for some, pain medication abuse leads to
> heroin." [3]

Living in an addicted society...whether alcohol, drugs, shopping, sex, gambling, fast foods, sugar, caffeine, nicotine...all of these addictions, possessed by many of the people living in our communities, portray extremely harmful modeling for our children.

3. Unhealthy Diet.

Not much has to be said about the dietary habits of our society or our children. Corporations take no responsibility and sabotage healthy eating habits when they advertise high sugar content products like sodas and breakfast cereals, or fail to advise us that their non-sugar products contain cancer-causing sweeteners. Adults who have coffee and donuts for breakfast, eat fattening lunches and overeat at the dinner table are part of the reason why our nation has so many cases of heart disease and cancer, the top two diseases in our country that lead to death.

The Cost to Society

The annual health costs related to obesity in the U.S. is nearly $200 billion, and nearly 21 percent of medical costs in the U.S. can be attributed to obesity. [4]

---

4. Media Dysfunction.

Advertisements create the desire for the continual purchase of products. Many of the movies shown in theaters are violent. Television comedy shows are disrespectful and encourage bullying. Most of the games you can buy for your TV are war games or games that encourage violent behavior. Our news media dwells almost exclusively on bad news; President Obama spoke recently about "...a saturation of news..." that keeps horrifying news foremost in our minds for high ratings. [5] Constantly being a witness to distressing information keeps us in a continual state of unease, hostility, and aggression.

5. Ineffective Leadership.

Take a moment to identify your modern-day heroes and you will be unable to respond with a name like Churchill, Roosevelt, Dr. Martin Luther King, Jr. or Albert Einstein. Who are the leaders we look up to today? You may rightly consider your father or mother, or someone close to you. But who are the national or global leaders we admire? Can you name more than two? The chances are you cannot; nobody can. We lack the visionary leadership necessary to move our lives forward.

6. A Lack of Good Paying Jobs.

Our economy has been sluggish since 2008. Our nation's

middle-class has been struggling with rising costs and frozen salaries. Inflation has increased costs by more than 20% in the last decade. The cost of college has gone through the roof, and we have seen gas prices jump as high as $4.00 per gallon. Jobs that support families are hard to find and in many two-parent families, both parents must work to make ends meet. Single-parent families and low income families must depend on the limited paychecks their teenage children can bring home. "Teenagers drop out of high school for all sorts of reasons: lack of motivation, little support from parents, poor academic performance. But for some low-income students, the decision to leave is purely economic. Many are going to work so they can start making money to help their families." [6]

The Number of Homeless Children Continues to Rise

"So many families are living on the edge of poverty, that one little setback can push them into the abyss of homelessness. A new report released Monday shows that about one in 30 American children was homeless at some point last year. That's about 2.5 million kids, and an 8 percent increase to "an historic high," according to the study from the National Center on Family Homelessness. Just over half are younger than six years old.

NBC News, November 17, 2014

7. People with Towering Debt.

The debt crisis is a serious national issue. The average household has $129,579 in debt; $15,355 of it on credit cards. [7] While it's true that some debt can strengthen a financial position (a mortgage, a car loan), in the last 12 years income growth has lost pace with the rise in the cost of living. Since 2003 the median household income has increased by 26%, but in the same time food costs have increased by 37% and medical costs by 51%. [8] Once a person becomes a victim of debt, it is very difficult to overcome.

The Cost to Society

The average American with a credit card owes $7,950 in revolving debt. [9] This is an average, and many people are trapped in revolving credit card debt, paying high interest rates that deny their family long-term financial health.

---

8. An Epidemic of Bullies.

We usually think of a bully as the angry kid on the playground, but this is not the whole truth. Most people have a bully in their life, or more than one. There are adult bullies at work; it could be your boss or a coworker. Customers can be bullies. School principals and belligerent school secretaries or custodians may have attitudes that create fear. A wife or husband can be a bully, a neighbor, and a doctor, lawyer, or other professional may behave with hostility. Bullying behavior is more rampant than people admit, given our culture of negative media, violent TV and movies, poor dietary habits, and the general frustration that's a part of living in a dysfunctional society.

9. Self-Absorption.

We live in a culture where most people are highly self-absorbed. Most people are interested more in themselves than others, focused on their physical appearance, self-gratification, buying material objects, and making a lot of money. Our political, social and economic systems are centered on rewarding an individual's achievements, often over monetary gain. People absorb the endlessly repeated messages that define themselves with what they have and how they compare to others. Our heroes are the celebrities in Hollywood, sports, and music, and we are encouraged to emulate their often shallow successes.

10. Loneliness and Disconnection.

People in other countries appear more involved with their neighbors, sharing their lives more freely with each other. In the United States we maintain superficial relationships with our neighbors and isolate ourselves with privacy. Most families do not live with their elders; most people are lonely and feel disconnected, possibly explaining the escape addiction offers.

11. A High Divorce Rate.

About 40 – 50% of the marriages in the United States end in divorce. A failed marriage is a tremendous hardship on the couple's children, and they experience accelerated stress and feelings of inadequacy that can result in disrupted lives and difficult relationships of their own as adults. With so much emotional pain, it becomes clear why many children struggle in school and favor the media and the glorified but shallow celebrities.

> ### The Cost of Divorce
> "One researcher determined that a single divorce
> costs state and federal governments about $30,000,
> based on such things as the higher use of food stamps
> and public housing as well as increased bankruptcies
> and juvenile delinquency. The nation's 10.4 million
> divorces in 2002 are estimated to have cost the
> taxpayers over $30 billion." [10]

12. Focusing on the Material.

We live in a capitalistic society where material objects such
as the size of your home and big screen TV are measures of
personal success. The car you drive, the clothes you wear, the
possessions you own, the vacations you take, the restaurants
where you eat, and the money you spend are either applauded
or condemned.

13. The Two Main Diseases.

Heart disease and cancer are the two leading causes of death
in the United States today. Over 600,000 people die of heart
disease each year because of medical conditions and lifestyle
choices that stem from diabetes, obesity, poor diet, physical
inactivity, and excessive alcohol use. Over a half million people in
the United States die every year from some form of cancer, the
second leading cause of death.

14. Our Toxic Environment.

It's no secret that our environment continues to be polluted.
Progress has been made, but the news is still full of stories about
the pollution of our air, water, and foods. The use of plastics and

pesticides, changing weather patterns, the steady extinction of species, and coal and petroleum versus alternative energy are examples of how our nation and communities are confronted with toxic conditions.

Our primary goal:
We want to build a healthy person.

Summary

As you can see, and without surprise, there are many critical factors eroding the quality of life for the people of our nation. Each of these is its own separate crisis, and the combined effect of these debilitating circumstances is contributing to the rapid decline of our society. These conditions have an overwhelmingly negative effect on our nation's children, which is considered in the next section.

The Effect on Our Children and Youth

The effect is catastrophic. Our children and youth are victims of our toxicity. We don't have thriving inspired students; on the contrary, the conditions in our society are devastating their lives. Here is a recitation of the more common misfortunes plaguing today's children.

- Students are bored with school because their classes are not relevant to either their interests or their perceptions of what will be useful.

- We have a very large dropout rate, and dropouts from middle school and high school enter the workforce with limited employment skills, likely to become involved with illegal activities that results in prison time.

- Many of today's youth glorify drinking and drugging and thus adopt these harmful practices, leading to addiction and compromised health.

- The school-to-prison pipeline is "···an epidemic ···plaguing schools across the nation···" [11]

- Adolescents are prone to making poor decisions such as befriending the wrong crowd, neglecting their school and home responsibilities, and engaging in risky behavior such as drinking, drugging, and having unprotected sex.

- Babies are having babies, with over 500,000 unintended teen pregnancies each year in the United States. [12]

The Cost to Society:
In 2010, teen pregnancy and childbirth accounted for at least $9.4 billion in costs to U.S. taxpayers for increased health care and foster care, increased incarceration rates among children of teen parents, and lost tax revenue because of lower educational attainment and income among teen mothers. [13]

- Teenagers become hostile when they seek independence from parental control.

- Over 31% of children in the U.S. between the ages of 10 – 17 are overweight or obese. [14]

- Suicide for children and youth ages 10-24 is the second leading cause of death, and each day in the United States an average of over 5,000 suicide attempts are made by children in grades 7-12. [15]

- 44% of all rape victims are under the age of 18. [16]

- Only one in four adolescents receives the recommended amount of one hour per day of physical activity.

- Few adolescents set goals for personal achievement or have the self-discipline necessary for healthy social, physical, or academic development.

- Adolescence is recognized as a time when most teenagers are self-absorbed and narcissistic, which appears as egocentric and selfish behavior and contribute to the disharmony of family relationships.

Are these outcomes the results we desire as a society and a nation? Are these our highest expectations for the health and well-being of our children? Do we want to live in a community and nation where these behaviors and experiences are commonplace? Of course not. It's time to ask ourselves how we got here and why today's school system has been unable to build a healthy person.

The History of U.S. Public Schools

This section is included merely to illustrate the original intention of the public schools and how our current school system came to be.

For hundreds of years, most learning happened in the home; parents taught their own children the skills and moral values they believed; wealthy families hired private tutors. The Puritans saw the need for public education and established schools that taught reading, writing, math, and reinforced their social and religious core values. [17]

In 1805, just 22 years after the end of the Revolutionary War, the New York Public School Society was created to provide education to the children of poor families. The program was based on a system in which one teacher was in charge of hundreds of students; this master teacher gave lessons to the older or smarter students who then taught the younger or weaker students. Discipline and obedience were key qualities, providing two essential factors desired by factory owners. [18]

Our schools are similar to the foster care model. Children are placed in a class for a year and then move on. They stay in a school for a few years and then move on. When they become 18 years old, they are pushed off the cliff into the adult world...which is when they need the most guidance and support of all.

In the 40 years before the Civil War, the number of farms declined and people moved to the cities; people found work in the factories. In the 10 years before the Civil War, over 3 million immigrants arrived, and factory owners needed the public schools to provide a docile workforce. [19]

"Employers in industry saw schooling as a way to create better workers. To them, the most crucial lessons were punctuality, following directions, tolerance for long hours of tedious work, and a minimal ability to read and write. From their point of view (though they may not have put it this way), the duller the subjects taught in schools the better." [20]

Eventually compulsory education became the law, and administrators began developing a curriculum of their choice without concern for losing children and funding. Parents began to lose their influence over the content, and over the years, schools became more subject to politics, more bureaucratic, increasingly separate from family priorities, and generally without moral content. [21]

Schools also became a good resource for teaching children about patriotism and creating the mentality for becoming soldiers. The curriculum included material that honored the moral virtues of the founding fathers and the nation's leaders, and promoted the importance of defending the homeland from enemies. [22]

Yes, there were also reformers who believed that children should be protected and educated with the skills and abilities that would help them become competent citizens with good character. Many of these caring educators also had their own agenda about competence and good moral behavior. Children should learn Latin, mathematics, the sciences and other curricular influences that would make them into scholars. [23]

This is generally how our current school system developed. We have compulsory education for ages 6 – 17 with a state standardized curriculum that includes six subject matter areas. English and mathematics, the age-old 3Rs of Reading, 'Riting, and 'Rithmetic, are considered the essential core, with a recent emphasis on science because of its multiple uses.

Education reform continues to this day within a tangled web of controversies about, to name only a few, student learning objectives, textbook development and selection, program funding, teacher training, the 180-day school year, making education relevant, the inclusion of children who need special education, are behaviorally challenged, require immigrant language support, come from low income homes and need breakfast and lunch programs, and student assessment..

"Our best intentions for changing the factory model will fail as long as our efforts culminate in the calibration of our students to factory standards for the college admissions process or the workplace.

More than our schools, our social expectations need disrupting. Our definitions of success and happiness need a paradigm shift." [24]

As with most bureaucracies, our current public school institution is cumbersome, ineffective, wasteful, and harmful to the people it intends to serve.

Billions of dollars are spent annually to sustain a system that is not working, which will never work, which does not accurately reflect the desires or needs of its constituents, and which is detrimental to the quality of life it seeks to assure.

The public school system is failing because it:

- Does not deliver what it promises, which is irrelevant anyway.
- Is modeled upon a set of expectations that is antique and no longer essential.
- Doesn't even have a clue about the right target.

Our primary goal:
We want to build a healthy person.

The next section reveals why parents, religious organizations, and community agencies are equally ineffective with building a healthy person.

Our society can NEVER improve as it is now.

The change we need can never come from our current political and social systems. Many people of influence in our communities, states, nation, and the world are book-smart but completely deficient in the qualities that heal and unite.

Our teachers, who should be building a healthy nation, are off-target from their true purpose, which is instilling positive life-long qualities in children during their formative years.

Schools and teachers are capable of making the significant changes we need when we shift their focus to building healthy children.

If Only...

When we think about raising healthy children, we often think of the role and influence of parents, religion, and the community. Unfortunately, all three of these resources are incapable of building a healthy child. Here is a review of why they, like the public school system, are also failing.

Parents.

Most people believe parents have the responsibility for building a healthy child, and indeed, we wish it were so. The fact is most parents are simply unable. The majority of parents are in survival mode, living day-to-day and working to pay ever-increasing bills. Most families are also dysfunctional in some way, living with unresolved issues affecting the entire family.

Some families have an adult who is addicted to drugs, alcohol, or gambling. Some families live with abuse. Many families are single-parent families, or children are living with a grandparent custodian. The adults may be unemployed or underemployed, creating unending anxiety about having enough money to provide food under a safe roof. Most families don't have time to practice good parenting, and frankly, the vast majority of parents were never taught how to be a good parent...so the unhealthy family dynamic keeps repeating.

The Church, Synagogue, Mosque or Temple.

The religious institutions in our communities are also broken. Perhaps at one time it was a good idea that religious leaders would lead the community, but today religion does not unite people. Every community has a number of different congregations, and this fragments the population.

In addition, organized religion is not usually a strong influence in the lives of people. Attendance is sporadic and thin, and few children are engaged. The significance of religious practice has become slim, with attention given mostly on holidays or for family events like weddings and funerals. Religious institutions in today's society are not capable of building a healthy person; their influence is slender.

The Community.

The community has resources that can serve children, but they function independently of each other. The Big Brother and Big Sister programs are not coordinated with the Boys and Girls Club, boy scouts and girl scouts, after-school sports programs like Little League or Pop Warner football, etc. Community service agencies that protect children and adults by providing assistance for a variety of urgent needs are also rarely coordinated. Besides, they are so completely burdened by the number of people and limited funding that they are incapable of contributing toward building a healthy person.

> "The first step toward change is awareness. We cannot change what we do not realize needs changing." Michael Reist, author of "What Every Parent Should Note About School".

What's Left?

This brings us back to the schools, but we have seen that in their present form schools are incompetent and not even pointed in the right direction. Besides, schools have never accepted the responsibility of building a healthy person, and instead they are relying on parents who are ill-equipped to fulfill this need.

- Schools are teaching different levels of 2 + 2, Jack and Jill, and C-A-T.

- Schools are breeding grounds for bullies.

- Schools, for the most part, only focus on academics, not the whole child.

- Schools serve unhealthy food in the cafeteria, classrooms, and at gatherings.

- Schools fund the band-aids of metal detectors, security guards, more counselors and more vice principals.

- Schools staff classrooms with one teacher for 25-30 students.

- School classrooms have a wide range of student abilities, backgrounds, and challenges that diminish teacher effectiveness.

- Schools impair children who want to learn by teaching to the classroom average.

- Schools are still teaching like it was the 1800s.

- Schools are spending huge amounts of money for only minimal results.

This is the current situation. We either allow it to continue and get worse, or we accept the idea that a massive change is needed. Sooner or later the system will become so broken it will fall apart. However, we are still at a crossroads where changes can be made that can turn this debilitating situation around and bring sanity and inspiration back to public education.

The schools are focused on the wrong target.

Plain and simple.

There is a warning, though.

To make a change this massive requires people with courage and foresight.

The change itself will not be difficult.

The difficulty is in being willing to make the change.

Building a healthy person means that the current system cannot stay the same. A community of healthy people cannot live in the communities we now have.

By turning this page you are willing to learn about a better future for our children and ourselves, and have the courage to co-create a meaningful, connected and wholesome life for everyone.

Part 2
What Children Really Need

Part 1 focused on the current situation and explained why the educational system we now have is incapable of producing quality outcomes. Part 2 presents a conceptual overview about what children really need to live satisfying and productive lives. We know that learning various forms of how to add 2 + 2, read Jack and Jill, and spell C-A-T are not essential to living a contented life that has healthy, self-defined meaning.

The next section proposes the circumstances and qualitative characteristics that will result in a life that is truly worth living. Part 2 presents the three most important categories for building a healthy person (the Foundation), explain the most important qualities a person can develop in order to connect with other people and live a satisfying life (First Floor), and explores the high quality and inspired educational outcomes that now become achievable (Penthouse).

When you have finished reading Part 2, you will:

- Know the three important categories necessary for building a healthy person.

- Have a strong understanding of the 10 important qualities that every healthy adult enjoys.

- Discern the difference between the experience of a below average educational experience and an inspired educational experience.

- Be familiar with the concept of a life coach.

- Realize that current public school expectations are irrelevant.

- Recognize that new public school outcomes are needed.

- Understand why outcomes for students should have more value for a child's life than simply building good academic skills.

- Support the idea that public schools should build good people, and not limit a child's education to only academic learning.

- Accept the idea that every child would be better served with an individualized learning program instead of being in a classroom that is irrelevantly based on a child's age.

- See the value of educating children based on their eagerness to participate in groups that motivate them to learn.

The Foundation

As everyone agrees, nothing can be accomplished without a strong foundation. The foundation is the first and most important part because without one, anything built upon it will be lost. Here is the blueprint for establishing the foundation that is essential for building a healthy person, a person who becomes a content, knowledgeable, and compassionate adult. These three elements will create a foundation that provides a child with the best opportunity for growing into healthy adulthood.

Our primary goal:

We want to build a healthy person.

---

1. Family and Extended Family (10 Points). A child's family is one of the most important parts of a child's development, if not the most important part. The family has a significant influence on the development of the child, imprinting patterns, beliefs, and practices that often become the primary operational codes for the child's entire lifetime. We are so deeply imprinted by what occurs in the first few years of life that we often have no idea why we think, or feel, or behave in the ways that we do without serious personal work over many years.

A supportive family is the most important factor in a child's life...father, mother, uncles, aunts, grandparents...and an extended family of good friends who truly care.

As engineers, we also understand that in most cases, the child will need support beyond the immediate family. The immediate family is seldom proficient with meeting early childhood needs because of the family's economic circumstances, or because the family has not had an effective family experience themselves. Our engineering plan includes extended family support from the school and community so the family receives what it needs to support their child's growth. In a very real sense, our engineering plan agrees that "it takes a village to raise a child". Everyone needs people around them who are caring and knowledgeable contributors, especially when raising a child in a healthy manner. The engineering plan includes a system that supports, engages, and enhances every family in the ways that are needed.

"I would have been just as screwed as most of my high school friends if not for my parents encouraging me to learn important, useful stuff outside of school." Scott M., college student.

2. Role Models (10 Points). It's natural that children look to their parents and other members of their family as role models. Children often assume the roles of those they see around them and mimic behavior and attitudes. As you know, this is sometimes good and sometimes not. As children grow older, their social connection with peers becomes more commanding, as does their acceptance of the behavior and attitudes they observe in the media. Unfortunately, the media is almost entirely unsupportive of good role modeling, as it is focused instead on sensationalism. In addition, a child's peer group may or may not be a good influence depending on the members of that group.

Because children will adopt behaviors and attitudes of those around them, it is essential that children have access to positive role models that can channel healthy behaviors and attitudes to impressionable hearts and minds. It is critical that children interact with peers and older children who are good influences, and it is also a necessity to have a celebrity role model / life coach who can inspire the behavior and attitudes we promote.

> Children need good role models, men and women who inspire healthy positive behavior. Who are your child's role models? Who do they look up to? Who do they take their advice from?

A celebrity life coach is a new idea that can have a tremendous impact on children's lives. To understand this concept better, let's pretend you were going to attend a two-hour seminar on child growth and development, and an expert in this field was going to make the presentation. The expert has the credentials and the experiences to speak knowledgeably and provide terrific insight...but the reality is even the expert's mother would be reluctant to attend. This is the status quo, and it's been going on for decades. When schools offer parenting classes, only the usual two or three parents show up, and they are the ones who are positively involved in their children's lives and attend all the school's functions.

On the other hand, if you had a celebrity like Joe Montana, the NFL superstar, give a talk about the exact same topic, you would pack the building and have standing room only as the audience listens closely to his every word. If Joe was at your school, parents would pour into the building to speak with him about parenting···and other important topics that would benefit their own children, all the students, and the entire school.

Instead of providing good role models, schools do the opposite of what a healthy child-engineer would do. When kids need someone to guide them the most, schools bring in security guards, metal detectors, more counselors, more vice principals...

Children need someone to look up to...or they are likely to stray in an unhealthy direction.

Whether we like it or not, for whatever psychological reason, celebrities always capture the interest of children and their parents, and these celebrities have a huge influence on the potential for creating healthy relationships and partnerships between children, parents, and the community. Our engineering plan requires the presence of a role model and life coach of good character and compelling stature from as close to birth as possible until the child is 25 years old; this range will be explained later.

The life coach will not be bogged down with teacher duties but will have the sole purpose of being a positive role model who develops friendly relationships between the children and the people in the school and community. In essence, the life coach becomes a big brother or big sister, bringing out the best in people and motivating them toward healthy behaviors and attitudes.

"Every child deserves a champion, an adult who will never
give up on them, who understands the power of connection
and insists that they become the best that they can possibly
be." Dr. Rita F. Pierson, educator and motivational speaker.

3. Hobbies and Interests (10 Points). The third essential
element for the foundation of a healthy person is a set of
activities that stimulate and engage the child. The last thing
we want are children, or adults, who are married to the control
panel of a video game. Every child must be exposed to a wide
variety of interests that have the potential for invigorating their
mind and their emotions. By finding a healthy interest, a person
has the opportunity to connect with other people, young or old,
with similar interests. Enjoying an activity, whether it is remote
controlled airplanes, quilting, raising animals, flying kites,
swimming, woodworking, model trains, beaded jewelry, stamp
collecting, or painting, etc., all open the door for social
interaction and being curious about the world, which is the third
essential piece to establishing a solid foundation.

Children love to play, and learn best by playing...

Offering a variety of clubs, groups, and teams doing
activities that kids want to do is the best way to motivate
them to succeed in their academic studies.

Let's move from the Foundation to the First Floor and discuss
the 10 indispensable traits that every healthy person must have

to enjoy a contented life as an active member in a nourishing community.

The First Floor

There is no mystery or secret here. All of these elements are a matter of common sense. These are the most essential components a child needs to develop during the formative years and which will provide him or her with the best chance for a fulfilling life into their 20s, 30s, 40s and up to their 80s.

As you read the following 10 traits and characteristics, you will quickly agree that these attributes are significantly more important to the establishment and development of a healthy adult than all the labors expended by the public schools in their use of the 10,000+ hours squandered in teaching academics.

Remember that these skills will be necessary every day and throughout the course of a healthy person's life, which will extend about 60 years beyond the age of 25 when the child achieves his or her adulthood and independence. These are skills that are relevant to living a decent and satisfying life, and necessary for exerting a positive influence on the world so it is a better place to live than when they were born.

The 10 Indispensable Traits

1. Kindness and Compassion (8 Points). The most important of all is showing kindness and compassion in word and deed. Some people have a natural propensity for this. Many others are too busy or too preoccupied to be heart-centered in all their interactions. There is also a portion of our population that takes pleasure with hurting others, and these are the bullies, people who have been damaged and must be contained and given appropriate education and nurturance. The current educational programs in the schools barely scratch the surface and anti-bullying programs have no lasting effect.

Many adults are highly deficient in this area, professional people like lawyers, teachers, salesmen, etc. Some businesses train their employees to bring customers in for a $19.95 oil change and won't let the customers leave until they spend $100 on unnecessary products and services. This is inappropriate and is an example of corporate bullying. Knowledge without compassion is dangerous. All the education in the world simply doesn't matter if you're not a good person. When it comes down to it, people don't care how much you know until they know how much you care. Acting with kindness and compassion is the most important behavior of all.

> "What wisdom can you find greater than kindness?"
> Jean-Jacques Rousseau, Philosopher

2. How to Save Money (8 Points). Everyone must learn how to save and invest their money. While the emphasis in our country is usually on making money, very few people know how to save their financial resources, spend wisely, and invest for their financial independence. Once you know how, it's not that difficult to do. Being astute with money and living within one's means will provide a healthy and secure future. We want and expect our children to become an economically responsible adult.

> "In the Industrial Age the ticket for success was to go to school, get good grades, and find a safe secure job for life. The rules have changed. You can no longer rely on your employer or your government to take care of you.
>
> Today, we are in the Information Age and more than job security we all need financial security. Unfortunately, our school system teaches us little about the subject of money. Our children will be required to learn much more than schools are prepared to teach them."
>
> Robert T. Kiyosaki, Author of "Rich Dad Poor Dad".

3. Responsibility (6 Points). Responsibility is an important quality, and children must be taught how to meet their obligations and be accountable for their actions.

4. Teamwork with All Types of People (6 Points). There are many different types of people, and it is important to know how to communicate and work together with everyone. Young and old, male, female, gifted, challenged, rich, poor, fast, slow, ethnically diverse...of the billions of people on Earth, none are the same...and yet we are the same in astonishing ways. A healthy adult is always capable of working together with a variety of different people.

People are living into their 80s. The 10 Indispensable Traits
are the skills they will need to live a good life for the 60+
years they will be adults. Memorizing the name of the
capitol of South Dakota just isn't that important.

5. Dedicated Work Ethic (6 Points). Only a few children are
taught the value of dedicated labor. It's valuable for a person
to learn that dedication to a goal will result in the pleasure of
achievement. Many children in our culture have an attitude of
entitlement, and to become a healthy adult they must learn how
to contribute meaningfully through commitment and persistence
toward achieving a worthy goal. There is also tremendous value
with teaching children the importance of working at tasks they
enjoy and tasks they do not. During the course of their 60 years
of adult life there will probably be numerous occasions when
they will need to perform disagreeable tasks effectively. These
students will not become employable if they don't learn how to
work hard and be a good team player.

> **"I believe 80% of my time at school
> was wasted academically."**
>
> Ann D., 2013 University of Washington graduate in finances.

6. Good Eating Habits (6 Points). Sadly, most children
develop very unhealthy eating habits that result in obesity,
eventually contracting heart disease or cancer in their later adult

years. Many doctors believe people die long before they should because of poor food choices. Poor diet is a death trap promoted by corporations that are selling food products that damage health; proper diet and exercise is the key to maintaining a healthy body, which is necessary for living in physical health for 80 years and longer.

7. Problem Solving Strategies and Good Choices (6 Points). We make hundreds of decisions every day, from choosing our breakfast to deciding when to go to sleep. It's important that children develop strategies that help them make the best decision possible. Whether it's deciding not to drink and drive, or making a plan to finish a task, or deciding the best way to fix a leak under the sink, a healthy person knows how to parse a situation and strategize ways to resolve any issue.

Everyone must be capable of developing a process that considers all the options and weighs the pros and cons for the most advantageous results...instead of regretting impulsive decisions or being unable to know how to approach a situation intelligently and with compassion.

What outcomes do we value?

What are the important results?

---

8. Leadership (6 Points). We don't have many good leaders because we don't teach people how to be good leaders. We need to teach children how to gather people and develop consensus, and how to make decisions that serve the group when there are conflicting opinions. Not only must we teach people how to lead well, but also how to work effectively in a group and support a leader who is working for the common good. Also, children sometimes join the wrong crowd because of the need to fit in with their peers, so children need to be taught how to be good leaders of themselves by also developing their self-worth.

9. Parenting Skills (6 Points). Kids having kids is all too common, with hundreds of thousands of unwanted teenage pregnancies every year. Learning parenting skills as a teenager is much too late; the best time to teach these skills is when children are young and showing an interest in caring for babies. By developing this understanding at an early age, children will quickly learn why they need to wait until they are able to care for child. Carrying around a 5-pound bag of sugar with a face drawn on it or a 10-pound baby doll that is programmed to cry for food every few hours is not a good replication of providing for the enormous financial, emotional, and mental needs of a child. Being a parent is a priceless experience, and with proper training and exposure, we could give birth to new generations of parents who are capable of effective and loving parenting.

What does a healthy person look like?

---

10. Creating Healthy Relationships (6 Points). Our lives are affected in innumerable ways through multiple relationships with siblings, parents, children, co-workers, neighbors, business associates, and romantic relationships. Yet, in so many instances these relationships experience conflict and one or both parties are disappointed and hurt. By learning about relationships, people can develop the skills that are necessary to promote and sustain multiple healthy relationships that augment the joys of a healthy life.

The Penthouse

Now we have reached the Penthouse where students are engaged in academics. It is into this area that our politicians and educational managers have been pouring all their resources... billions of dollars and billions of hours. However, our engineering plan for teaching children the academics they will need to pursue their life's purpose is not the same as that which is now in the public schools.

Because we know that children are not all the same, do not have the same sets of interests, learn at different levels and at different paces, have different strengths and weaknesses, come into themselves at different stages of their life, have different challenges that mediate or augment their abilities, have different family backgrounds, and different desires, expectations, and needs, our plan for this wide and diversified group of learners is to provide an individualized learning program for each child.

An individualized learning plan is an educational plan which is uniquely designed to fit the learning needs and abilities of each child. Instead of grouping children with widely diversified needs and abilities, frustrating the learning process and causing children to work either faster or slower than they are able, each child can develop the skills they need at their own pace.

At first, it might seem daunting to imagine creating an individualized learning program for every one of our nation's 50,000,000+ children in grades K-12, but as you will see in the next section it is not that difficult.

> There are many brilliant online individualized learning programs, such as the deservedly popular Khan Academy. These programs are the tools a child-engineer can use, but they are only tools. These tools will not be as effective as they could be until we change the system.

The individualized learning program has, at its core, a means for motivating children to want to learn, which is the essence of meaningful education. When people are forced to learn something, reluctance is often the first outcome. However, when a person has been motivated to want to learn something, the first outcome of their enthusiasm is attentive receptivity. Legislating the No Child Left Behind Act and its successor, The Every Student Succeeds Act, can never have the results the legislators want because legislating the same old style of education is destined to have the same old results.

Our proposal for a comprehensive individual learning program incorporates motivation as its key tenet, so children are engaged in the learning process by personal desire, not by legislative demand. Take a moment to think about what motivates you. Are you more likely to do something because you're told to do it or because you are motivated to do it? When you become engaged because there is a meaningful reward, the task is completed more quickly and with pleasure.

One size does not fit all.

It's the same thing for children. Once you find the way to create interest and enthusiasm for learning, there will be no stopping them from learning everything you wish. It's true that not every child will want to learn trigonometry or will be enthralled by chemistry or physics, but if we really want to see reading, writing, and math scores jump, if we really want to ensure that all students have a basic understanding of science and history, if we really want children to value the arts, physical education, and health, we can teach these important and wonderful concepts, behaviors, and attitudes when we connect with a child's motivation. We'll explore this topic further in the next section.

By the way, for the game we are playing about scoring points for your school, your school will earn 2 points each for reading, writing, math, and science programs, based on the expectations in the rubric in Part 5. The other courses will receive no points. Why? Because the schools don't value those courses as much; you can deduce this from the amount of funding.

Summary.

Part 2 explained how to strengthen a child's basic needs by establishing a strong Foundation composed of family and extended family, being able to interact with inspirational role models, and developing a child's engagement with hobbies and interests.

The First Floor, representing the essential skills a person needs to enjoy a productive and satisfying life, consists of the 10 Indispensable Traits; these traits compose the core of abilities necessary for being a healthy person living into their 80s.

The Penthouse, composed of the academics valued by parents and schools, can now be taught with complete success because the academics are in their proper sequence and students, as you will see, are motivated to learn. With this new system in place, children's assessment scores will soar in whatever area of learning a child is taught.

Part 3
Engineering a Healthy School System

In this section we contemplate the elements of a school system that's structured to provide a learning environment whose outcomes result in healthy people. The most important concepts are discussed, and a description is provided showing how the current school system can be restructured by making only three significant changes. In addition, an example illustrates how currently employed school resources can be reallocated so no new costs are incurred, yet the educational program becomes highly effective and results in learning outcomes of a higher degree.

When you have finished reading this chapter, you will:

- Know the nine important concepts that underscore the proposed public school restructuring plan

- See the value of "kids teaching kids" as an effective instructional method.

- Have a better understanding of why learning motivated by play significantly improves results area

- Become an advocate for the individualized learning program as a powerful educational process and as a means for liberating teachers for more meaningful instruction.

- Understand how the advances of the Digital Age can be applied in teaching children.

- Be familiar with the five components to the proposed restructured school system.

- Be able to explain the teacher-specialists' roles.

- Realize how reallocating a teacher-specialist's time can increase the impact and value of public school education.

- Appreciate how very few changes are necessary to the school facilities.

- Value an increased school day and increased school year.

- Acknowledge that the restructured use of the instructional personnel does not create any new costs.

- Possess the ability to explain the roles of the teacher-specialists in the restructured public school system.

The Nine Important Concepts to Know

Engineering a healthy school system that meets the essential formative needs and developmental skills of a healthy child requires a restructuring of the current educational system. Before we analyze the features of the proposed school plan, there are several important concepts we must review quickly.

1. Alternative Programs. As you know, there are schools in operation today that use a variety of educational theories that are having some success with their students. These include charter schools, homeschooling programs, Waldorf schools, Montessori schools, and other private schools that have structured their curriculum and school day to enhance the educational experience. Some of these programs are admirable and have great merit, but people who have studied these programs know they cannot come close to fulfilling the complete needs of most children...unless the parents are also developing the child's essential needs that were identified in Part 2.

2. No More Money. The plan outlined in this section will require no additional funding. We can stop pouring additional money into a dysfunctional school system; when we are aiming at the right target, the local school districts will be able to reallocate the money they are already receiving. It's likely that the local school district may even save money and have excess funds to augment the educational program in other ways. Imagine a school doing a much better job with less money.

**Schools don't need more money···
they already have enough.**

The funds just need to be properly reallocated.

---

3. Kids Teaching Kids. Teachers know that children are quite capable of teaching their peers. Every good teacher uses this strategy in their classroom already. In fact, you may remember from an earlier mention that New York City used this teaching method as long ago as 1805, probably one of the few practices in the 19th Century that would be wise to keep. We want to free the teacher from teaching to the class average and find ways for the teacher to instead guide and coach his or her students individually and in small groups.

When a teacher is tied down by 25-30 children with a wide range of multiple abilities and inabilities, we are in effect tying the teacher's hands and limiting an important resource that would otherwise be applied more effectively and efficiently.

4. Basic Knowledge. We want our students to learn the 10 Indispensable Traits, and we also want them to learn academic basics. We believe that every child should be able to read and write with proficiency, be able to use math to solve real life tasks, have a command of basic scientific knowledge, be familiar with important details about the history of our country and the world, have an appreciation for the arts, and be educated and physically active enough to have a healthy body and mind.

Of course we want children to read, write, calculate, be familiar with history, etc. Academics are important, but they are not nearly as important as the 10 Indispensable Traits.

These subject areas are all quite similar to the current curricular offerings in today's public schools. Remember, however, that proficiency in these areas is the organic outcome of children who are provided a strong Foundation and are growing properly under the influence of the 10 Indispensable Traits. Mastery of these subject areas will not be forced down their throats as it is in the schools today, but rather this knowledge will be absorbed rapidly because students are being motivated to want to acquire them.

5. The Motivated Learner. This is the most important element of the individualized learning program. As noted before, people do everything better when they are motivated. Our program's motivation stems from each child's interest in belonging to several activity groups. Anyone who has ever worked with children knows how excited children become when they are engaged in play. Play can take many forms, and it's important to realize that most learning occurs when people, children and adults, are engaged in play

- Abraham Maslow, American psychologist, 1908-1970. "Almost all creativity involves purposeful play."

- John Cleese, comic genius. "If you want creative workers, give them enough time to play."

- Roger von Oech, contemporary American creativity guru. "Necessity may be the mother of invention, but play is certainly the father."

- Carl Jung, founder of analytical psychology. "The creation of something new is not accomplished by the intellect but by the play instinct."

- Henri Matisse, French painter, 1869-1954. "Creative people are curious, flexible, persistent, and independent with a tremendous spirit of adventure and a love of play."

- Mark Twain, author. "What work I have done I have done because it has been play. If it had been work I shouldn't have done it."

- Jean Piaget, Swiss psychologist. "If you want to be creative, stay in part a child, with the creativity and invention that characterizes children before they are deformed by adult society."

- Pablo Picasso, Spanish cubist painter and sculptor. 'Every child is an artist. The problem is to remain an artist once he grows up."

- Albert Einstein, scientist. "To stimulate creativity, one must develop the childlike inclination for play."

Children will be motivated to learn the behaviors and the skills that are part of their development plan because they will urgently want to be involved in their hobbies and interests. When a child wants to be in the remote airplane club, or the basketball drill class, or the unicycle club, or the model train group, or the cupcake decorating class, you are speaking to a child at their most passionate level. In order to be in any of these motivating groups, the child must be doing well in their core areas of the 10 Indispensable Traits and their academic individualized learning program. The desire to participate in groups that are engaged in projects that appeal to their deep interest will provide the intrinsic motivation necessary to become successful in the areas we want them to learn for their own good in becoming a healthy adult.

6. The Individualized Learning Program. Everyone learns at their own pace, and an individualized learning program allows children to become accomplished learners in a manner that is best suited to their learning abilities. At the start of every school year, the curriculum director will assess the abilities of each child in every subject area and set learning goals for the year. Because the teacher is one of the engineers responsible for building a healthy child, the teacher is capable of analyzing a child's potential for academic growth.

The curriculum director will set the academic learning goals and standards of expectation that properly gauge the ability of the child to achieve. Of course, a child will meet, not meet, or exceed the expectations set for the year, and the director will monitor progress and adjust as necessary. In all cases, the student will be motivated to learn as thoroughly as possible; the pace of learning will depend on the child's abilities, the expectations of the teacher, and the motivation applied through child's desire to be involved in their selected interest groups.

Educators and some parents know that children are capable of learning much more than we ask of them. The true key to learning is the desire to learn. When we force students to learn material we think is important, resistance can overwhelm the best intentions.

When we motivate a person to learn by finding ways to capture their enthusiasm and help them find a way to develop in the areas that excite them, learning and enthusiasm for life becomes infinite.

An individualized learning program, fueled by a student's desire to participate in a special activity or hobby or sport, creates the environment where every child will be inspired to WANT to learn.

···To WANT to Learn···

We know some students will be interested in learning how to write competent essays···and some won't. Some students will get excited about quadratic equations···and some won't. Some students may actually be incapable because their abilities are limited, but no matter what their potential may be, every child will be taught as completely as possible. The strength of the independent learning program is that students can learn and grow with the best use of their time and abilities, and they are motivated by the excitement of participating in the groups that offer the development of exploring and enjoying their innate interests.

7. Life Coach. Another key element to remember is that there will be a life coach assigned to every school, and this person's responsibility is to spend time with each child, inspiring every girl and boy to develop positive attitudes, positive behaviors, and meet the expectations in their learning program. The significance of this component cannot be emphasized enough. People respond to the influence of someone they admire and respect, and in our contemporary society, celebrity-types in sports and other culturally popular categories have prestige and a tremendous impact on their admirers. Using this star-quality authority to leverage learning will result in highly positive advances among everyone in the school and in the community.

8. The Digital Age. Every child will have their own work station consisting of a computer connected to the Internet. Since we now live in the Digital Age, our schools need to be equipped with the technology that allows the restructuring of education so every child's capacity to learn is increased. As you probably know from your own experiences, there is now a vast amount of digital learning materials. We have access to libraries of videos created by experts in their fields who teach an almost endless variety of information in appealing ways on every topic from ancient Egypt to the exploration of space. There are learning materials available and appropriate for every ability level which can be used to free teachers from whole class instruction, allow the teacher to adopt the role of teaching resource and guide, and expedite independent learning.

> Do you believe technology can transform the
> educational structure we have today?

In addition to a wealth of video documentaries, there are also numerous online instructional programs that provide extensive and invaluable learning resources. Perhaps you've heard of the Khan Academy, referenced in the earlier part of this book, an online learning program that teaches math and science with interactive lessons that require students to observe and assimilate lessons, and then interact with instructional materials that assess their comprehension. With the teacher acting as guide and resource, programs like Khan Academy are completely effective and provide a major contribution toward the restructuring of the school system.

> Technology is a very important tool. It allows us to individualize learning and use one-on-one, small and large group instructional strategies to motivate children to want to learn.

9. Parents Joining Their Children. Another feature of the learning program is inviting and scheduling parents to work with their children at the student's work stations. Children often work better when their parents are observing and assisting. This also creates an important child-parent bond, and builds positive rapport between the parent, the teacher, and the school. A healthy relationship between the student, parent, and the teacher is an expected outcome. When parents become knowledgeable about what their children are learning and can see and contribute to the progress of their child, they become more capable of helping their child succeed.

A Toolkit for an Engineer of Healthy Children

Embellishing our metaphor and making the point more clear, the following list is an example of some of the tools an engineer would use to build healthy children.

Tools:

• Wrench:	Online math program
• Screwdriver:	Parents and extended family
• Hammer:	Positive role models
• Power drill:	Online science program
• Saw:	Jump roping club
• Needle nose pliers:	Local Boy Scouts chapter
• Work gloves:	Local Girl Scouts chapter
• Flashlight:	Community self-defense instructor
• Level:	Peer cross-age mentoring
• Allen wrench:	Local golf course
• Vice grips:	Local YMCA
• Tape measure:	Local 4-H group
• Pipe wrench:	Former students

Five Components for Restructuring the Current System

There are five components to the restructured school system:

1. The use of technology in support of the Individualized Learning Program.

2. A modified curriculum that offers motivational interest groupings.

3. The new role of the instructional staff.

4. Reorganizing the use of the school facilities.

5. A new school day and new school year schedule.

The first two components have already been introduced and will only be lightly revisited. The other three components will be reviewed in more depth.

1. The Use of Technology. Thanks to the Internet, the availability of inexpensive computer hardware, and the advent of a huge amount of quality online instructional materials, it is now technologically possible for students to be assigned a wide variety of programs that assess a child's abilities and provide a quality educational learning experience that build a child's skills to proficiency. The way we are currently using the blackboard or whiteboard and many of the textbooks is now obsolete. The days of needing a classroom teacher to explain long division to the whole classroom or even groups of children are over.

"I learned more in one day on an online math program than I did in a whole month at school." Donna V., 5th grade student.

---

2. A Modified Curriculum that Offers Motivational Interest Groupings. The way to inspire children to want to learn is by offering them the opportunity to participate in groups focused on activities and subject areas in which they are passionately interested. Whether it's being part of a dance group, building model rockets, learning how to bead or make candles, playing the drums, training animals or improving basketball skills, every child has interests or hobbies they want to explore and develop.

3. The New Role of the Instructional Staff. The current but now old-fashioned way of organizing the teaching staff in the elementary schools is having grade level teachers, which is the familiar structure of a teacher for kindergarten, first grade, second grade···etc. This system adjusts in middle school and high school to subject area specialists teaching different classes, such as an English teacher, a math teacher, etc.

We want to take this a step further so that in all grades, K-12, there are only subject area specialists, and they are teaching only their specialty. In the elementary school, students will no longer be organized by grade level, and instead will work at their work stations in their individualized learning program building their skills toward proficiency with students of different ages.

For example, here are the math specialist's assigned duties. The math specialist will:

A.   Oversee the online math program: The specialist will select the online programs that are appropriate for student learning, and will assure that the online programs are effective and efficient. Recommendations for improving the online instructional program will be made as needed.

B.   Work closely with the assessment specialist to ensure that students are developing their skills at the expected rate, and analyze how students can improve their progress, implementing changes that augment student growth in math.

C.   Teach students who are excited by mathematics, accelerating their skills. The math specialist may have several groups of gifted math students at different levels of knowledge and performance who are excited by mathematics and want to learn as much about math as possible. These students will be able to progress to the Advanced Placement (AP) level.

D.   Conduct large group seminars with the other students in the school to inspire student interest in mathematics. The purpose of the seminars is to show students how mathematics is an important part of adult life, and to ignite curiosity and enthusiasm for mathematics.

In addition, each school will have the following specialists, all experts in their fields:

- Reading
- Writing
- Math
- Science
- History/social studies
- Foreign language
- Technology
- Music
- Art
- Physical education
- Daily living

The intention for each of these subject-area specialists is the same as described in the math specialist example above. Because children of the same age do not have the same family or experiential backgrounds, the same sets of skills, or the same level of subject-area proficiency, grade level grouping does not make educational sense. Instead, having children at their work stations, engaged in quality online educational programs that effectively teach the skills they need to attain proficiency at an individualized pace, the instructional staff can be liberated to apply their talents and skills toward accelerating those students who possess the innate desire to excel in a subject area. In addition, the faculty now has the opportunity to conduct large group seminars for attracting student interest in their subject area, much like "Bill Nye the Science Guy" presents fascinating insights and inspires interest and engagement with science in children of all ages.

In essence, this is a reallocation of a teacher's time. In the current system, teachers are confined by the wide range of student abilities in their classrooms, which is organized by age groupings. Because not all students of the same age have the same abilities, teachers have a broad range of student interest and competency in their classrooms, restricting a teacher's ability to teach. Because the entire class must be brought along, the pace is ponderous. Once students are engaged in their individualized learning program, learning the skills they need through quality online instruction at their own pace, teachers will have the time to focus their talents more effectively in a new way for the benefit of all the students in the school.

Each of the specialist positions listed above represents a subject area; children will be taught the following subjects: reading, writing, math, science, history/social studies, foreign language, technology, music, art, physical education, and daily living.

4. Reorganizing the Use of the School Facilities. Current school facilities are completely adequate; it is just the use of some of the rooms that will need to be reorganized. A number of rooms will be dedicated as rooms that contain work stations with computers so students can access their online independent learning programs. Other rooms will be used, as they are, by the teacher specialists so they can conduct their small group lessons. The multipurpose room will be used for many things as usual, including the large assembly presentations by the different teacher specialists. Other rooms and outdoor areas will be used for the motivational student groupings so students may enjoy the classes, clubs or teams that focus on the hobbies and interests that students are excited about doing.

In all circumstances, student safety is paramount and adult supervision is mandatory. The rooms dedicated to work stations will be staffed by adult classroom assistants who will be present to respond to student questions, generally facilitate computer use, and manage student behavior as necessary. Students engaged in their individualized learning programs will also be able to access learning support from younger or older students who will be available and scheduled throughout the day.

As mentioned, peer-to-peer instruction is an effective teaching strategy that builds relationships and strengthens the school community, teaches children how to demonstrate kindness, and improves communication skills. The teacher no longer needs to be the first person students go to when seeking assistance. Students are not dependent on the teacher for their constant and complete instruction. In addition, trained parent volunteers will also be contributing to the supervision of these work station classrooms and to the educational process as learning coaches.

5. A New School Day and New School Year Schedule.
Once again, the school system is operating with archaic rules that do not fit the needs of families or the modern world. We need to improve the way we schedule the school day and the school year.

Wouldn't you like to know your children are in a safe and healthy learning environment while you are at work?

Improving the School Day Schedule: The school should be open from early in the morning to accommodate parents and provide academic and motivational classes until 6:00 p.m. for two reasons. The first reason is that we want to build the motivational classes into the school day so all students have time to attend them. The way things are today, many extracurricular activities and sports programs happen after the instructional day is over. This inefficiency limits the availability of these programs to all children; by including attractive programs like these in the school day, all children can be included.

Besides, many parents are unable to afford afterschool activities for their children; with an extended daily schedule, the opportunity for additional programs and homework time is built in. Otherwise, parents are often stressed-out by having to transport their children all over the place for practices, games, and tournaments, which is often a tremendous financial and burdensome time commitment on the family.

The second reason the school day should be extended is because this fits most working parents' schedules. Many parents leave for work early in the morning, and work until 5 o'clock; by the time they run a few errands and get home, it's after 6:00 p.m. Then it's time to make dinner and help their children with homework, creating a great deal of stress for the parent(s) and the family. By timing the end of the school day to fit the parent's schedule, students will always be supervised by an adult, and parent anxiety about their children being alone at home will be relieved. This adjustment eliminates latch-key kids, which is a service to children, parents, and the community. You've heard the light-hearted frustration about hot dogs in packs of ten but buns in packs of eight. Parents are frustrated and concerned when children are released from school at 3 o'clock yet parents can't return until 6:00; schools must serve parents better.

Keep in mind that children are not expected to be in school from 9:00 a.m. to 6:00 p.m.; this extended schedule is intended to offer flexibility for parents. As long as the child meets the state required annual minutes in the subject areas, the child is on course. This is true also for the extended school year.

Improving the School Year Schedule: This is another major inconsistency. Summer vacation originated when we had an agrarian society and children needed to be home helping on the farm during the summer months. When student learning stops for 10 weeks, a lot of progress is lost and teachers usually spend a good portion of the new school year refreshing student skills; this is typically lost instructional time. The school year should be reorganized so that vacation times mix well with instructional days. This may mean some version of a year-round school; there is a great deal of research about the value of this kind of scheduling.

Can you explain why kids are in school for 75%
of the annual number of work days?

$$180 / 240 = 75\%$$

It is also imperative that we increase the length of the school year. Currently an instructional school year is 180 days. Instead, schools should be teaching children 220 days. When you think about it, not only will students have the opportunity to increase their academic learning during these additional 40 days of instruction···an extra 18% of instructional time···but they will also not lose the progress they've made during an extended 2½ month summer vacation. On top of that, remember that children are going to be excited about staying in school because they will have access to the motivational classes, teams, and programs they desire. This will also cut back on the frustration parents have when figuring out what their children are going to do during the summer when parents are at work.

Remember, as long as a child attends school the required number of annual school days, the state mandate is met. This means parents have flexibility with complications that may need flexibility, such as with scheduling family vacation time.

Summary. The availability of computers and access to the Internet has become a game-changer in the last 10 years. Students, teachers, and schools are no longer bound by the restrictions that have been imposed by 19th Century-style educational limitations. We are living in a new era, and our schools need to use this technology so our children benefit in the multiple ways that are now possible. Individualized learning and restructuring the learning process, modifying the curriculum to motivate students to want to learn, liberating teachers so they can provide a higher quality learning experience for all students, and extending the school day and school year will all have an immense impact on the quality of education, and the quality of life for everyone.

Remember that our primary goal is to build a healthy person. When we break the barriers of keeping children in the box of age-level classrooms and one-size-fits-all instruction, and teachers are freed of constantly having to manage children, freed of teaching to the average, and released from having to manage constant behavior problems from children who feel left out, unappreciated, and unfulfilled, we can have a school system that develops children who are excited to learn, who feel appreciated and respected, and who want to be good students and healthy people because it is an integral part of their true nature.

An Example of Reallocating Resources

This segment will discuss the economics of restructuring a school. Let's take the example of a K-5 school with 300 students. A school this size, with six grades, typically has approximately 50 children per grade level, equivalent to about 25 children per class. This means there are two classes per grade level.

The Current School Staff:

- 12 grade-level classroom teachers, grades kindergarten through fifth grade.
- 1.5 special education teachers
- 1 Learning Assistance Program (LAP) teacher
- 1 English Language Learner (ELL) teacher
- 1 music teacher
- 1 physical education teacher
- 1 librarian
- 1 counselor
- 1 principal

This comes to a total of 19.5 teachers plus one principal.

Some schools have a part-time school counselor and foreign language teacher. The counselor is often the person who reviews student assessments and helps children and families with emotional conflict and accessing community resources. The foreign language teacher is sometimes a community person funded by the PTA to expose children to a foreign language, usually Spanish.

There are also support personnel, known as classified staff, who assist the principal and the teachers with managing the school and supporting instruction in the classrooms. A school of this size is likely to have one school secretary and a sufficient group of instructional aides working part-time in the 12 classrooms. There is additional classified staff in the cafeteria, and custodians, and bus drivers; their job assignments will not vary greatly.

Our focus is on the teaching staff, and demonstrates there will be no additional costs for implementing these significant instructional adjustments.

The New Designations of School Staff: The staffing requirements, and thus the costs, are unchanged. The new school faculty assignments also equal 19.5 teachers plus one principal.

- 1 reading specialist
- 1 writing specialist
- 1 math specialist
- 1 science specialist
- 1 history/social studies specialist
- 2 technology specialists
- 1 music specialist
- 1 art specialist
- 1 physical education specialist
- 1.5 special education teacher
- 1 individualized learning program and assessment director
- 1 daily living specialist
- 1 English Language Learner (ELL) specialist
- 1 librarian
- 1 foreign language specialist
- 1 principal

This comes to a total of 16.5 teachers plus one principal. This is three teaching positions less than the current typical teacher assignments of 19.5. With the capacity for three additional positions, two of these will be apportioned to the two life coaches assigned to the school, one male and one female. That leaves one extra position which is for the director of the motivational programs as explained below.

There will be twelve classified instructional aides, each assigned to an instructional classroom to serve students and teachers.

As you can see, staffing remains the same. In this example, the current school has 19.5 teaching positions; in the restructured school, the 19.5 positions have been modified to accommodate the new instructional program. By reassigning the teaching roles and expectations, there are no additional costs to the school. Costs have stayed the same, and now the school is capable of offering a significantly improved educational program.

A Brief Overview of the Instructional Positions. More than half of these 19.5 instructional positions were already described, but there are some new ones that are briefly defined below.

1. The reading, writing, math, science, and history/social studies specialist positions have been explained. These positions augment the school's educational program by allowing the specialists to develop the skills of students who have a natural inclination and possess the ability to increase their abilities to perform at the Advanced Placement (AP) level. Most of the students in these specialty classes will also be assigned to mentor and teach students who are working in their

individualized learning programs. Students can be the best teachers when put in the right situations, and this is also another way of developing leadership, kindness and compassion, relationships, etc.

As mentioned, the specialists will also do their best in group presentations to ignite the curiosity and inspire all students to develop an interest by making their subject area fun, and as real and practical as possible to demonstrate how their specialty **could lead to an exciting and worthwhile lifelong career.**

2. This is also true of the music, art, and physical education specialists.

3. There is no change for the special education teachers.

4. The English Language Learner (ELL) specialist will continue in his or her role helping children with a language other than English to acquire the skills they need to be successful in school.

5. The foreign language specialist will serve English-speaking students with learning another language. The community in the school can decide which language is most appropriate; in most cases, there is a need for English-speaking students to learn Spanish, though this may be just one of several foreign languages offered at the school. American Sign Language may also be an offering.

6. The technology specialist positions serve two purposes; they will ensure that students and subject area specialists are supported by the online learning programs, and they will also teach children interested in becoming technologically proficient

in various categories.

7. The daily living specialist will offer students a variety of experiences, teaching them how to repair items around the home and office, how to buy food economically and prepare meals, how to take care of a home and car, etc.

8. The librarian will fulfill the normal role of being a resource for students and specialists; however, there will be an emphasis on identifying digital materials that better serve the school's new focus on instruction.

9. The individualized learning program and assessment director will ensure that the online learning program is effective for all students. This director will review every student's learning program, and will monitor and assess progress.

Teacher-specialists are now able to accelerate student learning because technology is serving children in their individualized learning programs. Specialists can now provide assemblies that inspire children with the excitement of learning their subjects.

---

10. The two life coaches' roles have already been described. We want both a male and female so gender-specific issues can be addressed when necessary. All children in the school will have a life coach who takes interest in their well-being, guiding and supporting them through the years.

11. The director of motivational programs is responsible for the

programs that make this exciting and inspiring collection of experiences possible by inviting the community to participate, providing the scheduling organization, and assess and improve the programs for continued student interest.

Some of these clubs, groups, and teams will be staffed by teacher-specialists with an interest in promoting their subject area. For example, the physical education specialist may want to or coach a basketball skills club, or teach a unicycle group, or start a bowling team. The music specialist may want to organize a group that prepares for performances and takes field trips to local music presentations in the community.

Other clubs, groups and teams might be sponsored by parents and community members with special interests and hobbies they want to share. Some offerings, which have already been successful in public schools, are groups interested in pottery, animal husbandry, growing a vegetable garden, building a solar-powered car, knitting and quilting, creating an online interactive game, learning how to bake, building and flying kites, volunteering time at community service organizations, playing board games, starting and expanding collections, scrapbooking, etc. By bringing the resources of the community into the school, rapport is built between all participants in the school and the community, creating bonds between children of all age levels as well as adults and elders···contributing to the building of healthy people and a healthy community.

12. The role of the principal is largely unchanged. This person ensures that the new engineering plan is being provided effectively and efficiently by the faculty and staff, and supports all school participants with their learning programs and

integrating the school with the community.

13. There will also be several new classified positions or parent volunteer positions.

A. Our school will have an on-site and off-site job placement program. Children ages 5 to 11 can work on-site and children 12 and older can work on or off-site. A coordinator will make the arrangements.

B. A parent facilitator will follow a group of students throughout the children's educational time to facilitate parent support and interaction.

> Parents will be more completely involved in the daily operations of the school of the future.

Summary. The main intention of this section was to show that a reorganization of the instructional staff would not require any additional funding. A contemporary school of 300 children could be expected to have a teaching staff of 19.5 positions, and that same school, with a reorganized instructional staff, could accommodate a more stimulating and more productive educational learning experience with the same number of staff and without any additional cost.

Because the reorganized school would not be structured on grade-level and age-level distributions but would instead have a comprehensive individualized learning program for every child, teachers are no longer tied to teaching to the norm and instead are free to inspire all the students at the school in a new, creative way. By removing the harness of grade and age-level instruction, new positions can be created that satisfy important functions within the restructured school that can promise and deliver children who become healthy adults contributing to a thriving community.

The current public school system can be completely restructured by making only these three significant changes,

1. Using technology in support of the individualized learning programs,

2. Modifying the curriculum so motivational interest groupings can inspire children to want to learn,

3. Adjusting the roles of the instructional staff so teacher-specialists can teach their subject matter without interference, augmenting the educational experience for children who are eager to learn and stimulate others with the curiosity to learn more.

The other changes that will be necessary to support the restructure of the current public school system are minor managerial tasks.

Our society can NEVER improve as it is now.

The change we need can never come from our current political and social systems. Many people of influence in our communities, states, nation, and the world are book-smart but completely deficient in the qualities that heal and unite.

Our teachers, who should be building a healthy nation, are off-target from their true purpose, which is instilling positive life-long qualities in children during their formative years.

Schools and teachers are capable of making the significant changes we need when we shift their focus to building healthy children.

Part 4
Bringing It All Together

The average adult living in the United States is generally expected to live into their 80s. To enjoy the benefits of such a long life, there are certain attributes that can enhance the experience of living decades as an adult. Unfortunately, many people are highly deficient in these essential areas because these abilities were not developed during their formative years.

We have seen how most children do not receive a strong Foundation. Many children do not have the support of a strong family nor the benefits of an extended family that provide wholesome attitudes, beliefs, and behaviors for children to emulate. Role models for most children are based on what they see in the movies, on TV, and in many forms of media; these role models are often copied by their peer group, further integrating disturbing attitudes, beliefs and behaviors in their personalities. The result is that we have people in our country who are victimized by excessive addictions, unhealthy diets, an epidemic of bullies, a high divorce rate, and a toxic emotional environment, among other ills.

If there is to be meaningful change, it must happen in the public schools. The reason is simple. The public school system is the central hub for most children and communities, the place where most young people gather to be instructed in the skills and behaviors that are important for their lifetime···yet the public school system as we know it today is an abject failure. Graduates of the public school system, who have spent over 10,000 hours learning skills that are not completely relevant for a happy and successful life, are likely to experience decades of struggle trying to keep a roof over their heads, provide their children with the hope for a better future, and wrestling with relationships within their families and among their coworkers.

Many of these adults may be successful with the skills they acquired through the rigors of an educational system that's aiming at the wrong target. They may grow to become adults who are deficient in the essential areas of kindness and compassion, leadership, responsibility, etc., and may wind up causing great harm to others in their positions of influence as a judge, attorney, policeman, pastor, teacher, or politician. A great many of our so-called leaders excelled at the programs offered by prestigious colleges and universities, yet they are incapable of making a difference in the lives of our country's people to the degree that our society clearly needs. Our social system will continue to devolve with the negative influences of aggression, addiction, misplaced purpose, personal dissatisfaction, and the unhealthy attitudes, beliefs, and behaviors that form the daily reality of millions and millions of people in our country and around the world.

Who is going to break this horrific tragedy to our children and renew their hope for a meaningful and contented life?

No one believed it was possible to break the four-minute mile, but once Roger Bannister did, many more followed. We just need to show the politicians and the state education managers that a major healthy change is possible.

Are you contributing to the well-being of all, or only putting bandaids over this giant gash that is contributing to the downward spiral of our country, and causing great pain and suffering to present and future generations?

Do you believe it is time for a better life?

Are you willing to get involved in whatever capacity you have available so that you can change the outcomes that our current public school system and society is creating?

Would you be willing to support significant changes that will help your children or grandchildren have better lives?

If not, the chances are that the only changes you'll see will be a continual worsening of the situation···and the eventual collapse of our country and civilization.

However, if you are willing to be part of the change you know must take place, then you are invited to select one or more activities in Part 6 so you and many others, including your children and grandchildren, will have the opportunity to live a more complete and healthy life in a community that values kindness and compassion for everyone, and knows that a healthy person is the most important goal of the public schools.

Part 5
The Scoring Rubric:
How Well Does Your School Score?

Play the Game!

At the beginning of this book you were invited to assess the capacity of your child's school with providing the skills and abilities necessary for living a meaningful life as a healthy adult. Please follow the instructions below to determine how capable your child's school is with meeting this goal.

Scoring:

Foundation: 10 points each for providing the core of what a child needs.

Family and Extended Family: 10 Points.
Score 10 points if your school has a program in which 60% of the parents and/or extended family are involved in the school on an average of 2 hours a week tutoring their child and other children academically, or volunteering in motivational clubs; parents are connected with the children throughout their educational experience.

Score 0 points if the school has a PTA which involves a handful of parents meeting occasionally to discuss ways to support their children and teachers to raise money for field trips, assemblies, and additional classroom supplies; the school meets with parents twice a year at the fall and spring conferences.

_____ points

Good Role Models: 10 Points.
Score 10 points if your school has a role model program in place where kids of all ages are admiring and seeking advice from a person who assists them in all areas of wellness throughout the years. This person takes the role of a big brother/sister, mentor, and friend to the children and parents.

Score 0 points if your school has no program which unites all students; in most instances, children are feeding off each other and not looking up to a positive role model during their vulnerable middle and high school years. Instead, your child's school is hiring security guards and policemen to monitor the campus during school hours and/or installing fences and metal detectors.

___ points

Hobbies and Interests: 10 Points.
Score 10 points if the school offers 25 or more different activities throughout the week that bring together children and adults of all ages and like interests; students are allowed to leave their academic learning station to participate in these high interest and motivational activities. Each child is involved in at least three of these activities, and one must be musical.

Score 0 points if the school offers the traditional physical education and music program where the children are required by the state to attend one or two days a week, or are required to take an arts course. Students are not allowed to leave class to attend these motivational activities because they will miss out on the whole group instruction in the classroom.

___ points

First Floor: 8 points each for these two Indispensable Traits.

Kindness and Compassion

Score 8 points if the school has a program in which each child is required to volunteer two hours a week at school; this program also connects all children with the community for regular ongoing volunteer work.

Score 0 points if the school has a good character program that awards good citizens periodically through the school year.

___ points

How to Save Money

Score 8 points if 90% or more of the children in school have a long-term savings account set-up at a bank or credit union and are involved in various activities to increase their fund. Students are also involved in a school or community work program to understand how to make money and live within a budget. A curriculum teaches these strategies from the beginning of their educational experience through graduation, and is taught throughout the week.

Score 0 points if the school gives worksheets to children where they have to identify the value of U.S. currency and answer questions using money; some students are actively involved in Junior Achievement.

___ points

First Floor: 6 points each for the other eight Indispensable Traits.

Leadership

Score 6 points if the school has a program that involves 30% or more of the students in a peer or cross-age teaching program throughout the year. All students are involved in a leadership curriculum to gain leadership understanding and characteristics.

Score 0 points if the school has a student body government that meets once a month to discuss such items as dance decorations, booster club activities, and types of penalties for student misbehavior.

___ points

Responsibility

Score 6 points if 90% or more of the students are fully involved in an individualized learning program and taking responsibility for their personal learning development. A curriculum that teaches these strategies from the beginning of their educational experience until graduation is taught throughout the week.

Score 0 points if the teacher assigns work on a weekly basis for students to complete at home.

___ points

Teamwork

Score 6 points if students are engaged in a regular program taught throughout the school year on how to work together as a team, and how to meet the expectations of different role responsibilities. These teams build rapport and good communication, focus on setting and achieving goals, and are supportive of every team member whether the team succeeds or not.

Score 0 points if students occasionally collaborate in the classroom or are arbitrarily selected for physical education teams.

___ points

Dedicated Work Ethics

Score 6 points if your school sets weekly, monthly, and annual learning goals and objectives in collaboration with each student and the student's parents; a system of steady goal awareness and achievement guides the work and progress of each student.

Score 0 points if your school expects students to be grade level proficient, but less than 60% of the student population can accomplish this standard in every state-assessed subject area.

___ points

Good Eating Habits

Score 6 points if children in the school are eating meals daily that are made from an appropriate amount of fresh fruits, vegetables, and healthy home-cooked meals 90% of the time.

Score 0 points if students are eating donuts and sugary food for breakfast, and corn dogs/fries or cheese sandwiches for lunch.

___ points

Good Problem Solving Strategies and Good Choices

Score 6 points if all students are taught strategies to solve problems and make good choices. They practice these skills throughout the week as they are faced with numerous weekly choices. A curriculum to teach these strategies from the beginning of their educational experience until graduation is taught throughout the week.

Score 0 points if only students who have mild to severe emotional or behavioral issues meet with the counselor to discuss personal issues and problems.

___ points

Parenting Skills

Score 6 points if older children are interacting with younger children and taught the enormous resources (time and money) it takes to properly raise a child. A curriculum to teach these strategies from the beginning of their educational experience until graduation is taught throughout the week.

Score 0 points if the students wait until high school to take a home economics course where students are asked to carry around a 5-pound bag of sugar or a doll that is programmed to cry.

___ points

Healthy Relationships

Score 6 points if your school has a curriculum to teach about relationships; children are placed in situations each week to develop a better understanding about the nature of mature relationships from the beginning of their educational experience until graduation is taught throughout the week.

Score 0 points if children with emotional and behavioral issues visit the counselor to talk about how to handle anger and fear.

___ points

Penthouse: 1 or 2 points for each academic target.

Score 80% or more of the students score at or above grade level in the following areas: math, reading, science, history.

Score 0 points if 20% or more of the school scores below grade level.

___ points reading   (2 points possible)
___ points math   (2 points possible)
___ points writing   (1 point possible)
___ points science   (1 point possible)

_____ **Total points. (100 points possible)**

Check your results and see if your school is contributing to the downward spiral of a child's future.

How Well Did Your School Score?

A grade – 90 - 100 points.
You have a school system where 90% or more of the children have the best chance for living a content and meaningful adult life in which they are contributing to the greater good of all.

B grade – 80 – 90 points.
80% or more of the children will have a good chance for having a content and meaningful adult life that contributes to the greater good of all.

C grade – 70 – 80 points.
70% or more of the children will have a good chance to grow up and have a content and meaningful adult life that contributes to the greater good of all.

D grade – 60 – 70 points.
60% or more of the children will have a good chance to grow up and have a content and meaningful adult life that contributes to the greater good of all.

F – 60 points or less.
FAILED. Your school has failed if it scored less than 60 points. Students are very dependent on their parents and/or a mentor to help them weather the storms of life, and the school has little impact on the well-being of their future. Most students

will belong to a government-assisted financial program (welfare, housing, food stamps), will be addicted to drugs or alcohol, and many of the so-called successful children are highly deficient in kindness and compassion; some resort to selective bullying. As adults, the children of your school will be a burden to taxpayers and the government, and require subsidized health care.

"We must motivate ALL students to want to achieve higher standards, both intellectually and morally, despite the growing influence of an amoral popular culture that encourages consumption, not creation."

Tony Wagner, Author, Making the Grade: Reinventing America's Schools.

The Results of Your Assessment

How Well Did Your Child's School Do?

It is rare if a school scores higher than even 25 points. Most schools will earn some of the points represented by the Penthouse because this is the typical academic target most schools serve, but even scoring the full 8 points in this category would be a rare feat.

A few schools may score some points from the First Floor from among the 10 Indispensable Traits such as effectively teaching problem-solving strategies, and learning to work as a team. Perhaps one or two other elements might be taught, though these are likely to be treated superficially and not as an essential part of the school's program.

As for the Foundation, it will be absolutely amazing if any school offers a catalog of hobbies and interests that are used primarily to motivate children to take responsibility for the required academic learning of the school. Equally stunning will be identifying any school that uses positive adult role models as described in this book, or a school that effectively builds upon the foundation of a family and extended family.

The point is clear. Public schools are aiming at the wrong target and are not preparing our nation's children and youth for a meaningful life as a healthy adult. Even so, public schools are currently the best option available because of how completely they are integrated into our society and the lives of almost all American families.

If you agree with the premise and conclusions of this book, then I hope you will take some positive action. Please send this book to someone of influence, or better yet, visit with some of the school board members in your community and ask them to read and respond to this material.

Change is not possible...unless we all take responsibility for the change we owe our children.

The change must begin now, and you can start this change by committing to some of the activities on the next page and taking action today.

Part 6
What You Can Do Now

Change is needed, and it is needed now. The best way for something to begin is by beginning it yourself. The author of this book is very willing to make himself available for phone conferences and possibly for speaking engagements. Please contact the email address below if you would like to get in touch and explore the possibilities for establishing a school like this in your community.

> "Never doubt that a small group of thoughtful, committed citizens can change the world; indeed, it's the only thing that ever has." Margaret Mead

Here are some suggested activities worth considering to initiate change in your community:

1. Give this book to someone you know: a fellow parent, a school board member, the principal of your school. Ask the person to read the book and if they agree with the ideas, have them give the book to another person. Spreading the ideas in this book can begin a conversation that leads to change.

2. If you are a school board member and would like to know more about these ideas and how change can be implemented in your school district, please contact the author.

3. If your school district is looking for ways to improve its educational program, ask the school managers to contact the author for a conference call or a personal presentation.

4. If you are a parent and would like your child to attend a school like the one described in this book, it may be possible to start a private school in your community that uses the philosophy represented here. However, we really need a blueprint for the public schools because otherwise the significant social changes we need to make will never happen, and the public schools will continue to use the excuse of "We can't do that!"

5. If you are a person of influence and would like to fund a school that operates with the concepts found in this book, please contact the author.

> "Do not wait for leaders; do it alone, person to person."
> Mother Theresa

Contact Info: Matt W. Beck: OutofChaos12@gmail.com

Part 7
Addenda

More Online Videos You Must Watch

There are a number of excellent online videos available for you to explore. Watch a few if you can because they will expand your awareness of the problem and its solution. To watch these videos, go to YouTube and type in the link, or go to YouTube and enter the keywords in the title.

A. Children Can Perform at High Levels

Your school has children who can perform at these levels when given the opportunity, and many other children can perform at much higher levels than they are being asked. Why aren't we giving them a chance?

1. "6 Year Old Girl Is the Next Steph Curry!"
https://www.youtube.com/watch?v=oOaeY6CrF8I

Student comments:
- "I want to be her." First grader.
- "Can you come over and help me do those basketball drills?" Kindergarten student.

2. "GHHS Talent Show 2013-Cary Super Skippers"
https://www.youtube.com/watch?v=e9OEFqMqFBM

Student comments:
- "I've seen older kids jump rope. Can they teach me how?" First grader.
- "Can we start a jump roping club at our school?" Fourth grade student.

3. "6 Year Old Shows Mental Math."
https://www.youtube.com/watch?v=uyR1eSD6uXE

Student comments:
- "I'd like to try that." Second grader.
- "If you could show me how, I could do that." Third grade student.

B. Children Respond to Motivation

When our schools are restructured and teachers have more flexibility to teach in different ways, there will be more opportunity to develop children into good students and healthy people. Personal motivation should extend throughout the length of an adult life and we just need to help them find their joy in living.

1. "Becoming Better Than Yesterday"
https://www.youtube.com/watch?v=N2WVHIau77Q
Nobody can do better than you when you truly dedicate yourself.

2. "The Importance Of Motivating School Children For A Successful Future"

https://www.youtube.com/watch?v=JWWVD8lUWVA
You have dreams, and dreams are beautiful.

3. "The School of Rock", 2003.

This is a good movie to rent; and it clearly makes the point!

C. Children Need Good Role Models

One of the most effective ways we learn is by observing others. When our children have healthy role models, they emulate healthy characteristics. If we don't provide role models, our children will find their own role models through the messages they see on television, in the movies, and among the galaxy of misbehaving music, sports, and movie stars. Which do you prefer?

1. "The Seven Male Role Models Every Child Needs For a Healthy Upbringing"

https://www.youtube.com/watch?v=yuqesXL0IOE
There are seven types of men and each brings a healthy value children need.

2. "Rita Pierson: Every kid needs a champion"

https://www.youtube.com/watch?v=SFnMTHhKdkw
We all need someone special to lead us to the best of ourselves.

3. "What makes a great healthy role model?"

https://www.youtube.com/watch?v=N_e0oAd_TuQ
Young children discuss the role models in their lives.

D. Our Children's Financial Future Is Challenged

Whether we like it or not, our world revolves around money, Money, and MONEY. Most adults struggle with living within their means, and your child's financial future could be in great danger unless steps are taken now. Children need to learn how to take care of themselves financially when they become adults. When you look at the news today, you can see this is not happening. Also consider that the average cost to raise a child from birth to age 18 is about $250,000; when people have children and they can't afford that responsibility, they're putting a tremendous financial burden on society and those people who are providing for their families. 22% of all children living in the United States today are living in poverty. [25] 76% of all Americans are living paycheck to paycheck. [26]

1. "Dave Ramsey on Kids and Money"

https://www.youtube.com/watch?v=DTbLMPeKV98

"Signing up for a credit card doesn't make you an adult, it makes you a slave."

2. "Dream School: Dream Teachers - Suze Orman"

https://www.youtube.com/watch?v=yYTQ3xqYO7A

"I'm successful because I know who I am."

3. "9 and 10 Year-Olds Survive Suze Orman! - Ask Oprah's All Stars - Oprah Winfrey Network"

https://www.youtube.com/watch?v=lG2R23QVv5o

How many pairs of shoes do you need?

E. Technology is a Tool to Build a Healthy Child

In the last decade, technology has become a major influence in our society. Educators realize the value of computers and the Internet but have not been able to use these tools effectively and universally. Individualized learning programs can effectively teach children, allowing the expertise of the teacher to be used in more important ways. Online learning is a tool to help us build healthy kids.

1. "Peter Norvig: The 100,000 student classroom"

https://www.youtube.com/watch?v=tYclUdcsdeo
The ability of online learning to teach masses of people.

2. "Blending technology and classroom learning: Jessie Woolley-Wilson at TEDxRainier"

https://www.youtube.com/watch?v=o0TbaHimigw
Technology can increase the velocity of learning.

3. "Can Technology Change Education? Yes!: Raj Dhingra at TEDxBend"

https://www.youtube.com/watch?v=l0s_M6xKxNc
Three inspiring stories about how technology has advanced education.

F. Restructuring Education

Until we change the system, nothing will change. We can continue to throw billions of dollars at the current educational structure and all we will do is squander those resources, as well as more billions of dollars to deal with the problems of addiction, welfare, unwanted pregnancies, and joblessness we have created because we did not focus on the 10 Indispensable Traits of building a healthy person. The great news is that we can make the transition to an effective and healthy educational experience for every child if we are courageous enough to accept that what we have is not working. The change does not have to be gradual, either; we can start making these changes immediately. Do you have the heart?

1. "Ken Robinson: How to escape education's death valley"
https://www.youtube.com/watch?v=wX78iKhInsc
Our children are disengaged in school because education is going in the wrong direction.

2. "TEDxPhilly - Chris Lehmann - Education is broken"
https://www.youtube.com/watch?v=tS2IPfWZQM4
Children go to their 42 minute class, and their next 42 minute class, and their 31 minute lunch...

3. "TEDxAtlanta - Gever Tulley - Reimagining Education"
https://www.youtube.com/watch?v=upopmzRUe94
We need to stop trying to fix the broken system because we are just making it more broken.

The Real Hero Mentor Program

Several years ago I established the Real Hero Mentor Program at my school. The purpose of the program was to connect the children in my school and their parents with a local and well-respected celebrity. The celebrity I chose was Pete Kaligis.

Pete is now a football coach at the University of Wyoming, and is a former football player, as well as a former track and field athlete. Among his accomplishments is being an All-American shot puter, a three-time Rose Bowl Game participant, and he was also a starter for the 1991 national football champions at the University of Washington.

The program was a great success, and shows the positive power a good role model in the schools can have on all the children. Here are several of the comments this program received:
"I saw such a change in the kids, from being sarcastic, pushy kids, to kids who want to be great. I just can't say enough about Pete. He makes kids feel important." A parent.

"I think that Pete is the best thing that has happened this year. He really, truly helps kids who have some problems. He makes kids want to reach out to him because they want to be like him and be his friend. Also when he teaches us about drugs, he's serious, he doesn't fool around. He gets to the point and really makes you want to think long and hard about the causes that drugs impact on your body. He is also a fantastic gentleman, even if you don't know him, he will say hi to you in the halls and say to have a great day. Pete is an all around kids' hero!" An 8th grade student.

"I believe Pete Kaligis is a wonderful asset to our school program. As a mentor and role model to our middle school students, Pete has positively impacted the lives of many of our students. In general, the students look up to and admire Pete. His upbeat demeanor and respectful ways with the students have won them over. Additionally, Pete sets a tone that expects respectful and responsible behavior from the students. The students respond to his interactions with them in a manner which demonstrates their strong desire to connect with him." A middle school language arts teacher.

"Ever since Pete Kaligis came to our school, things have changed. There has been such a huge difference. I have noticed that he always puts others before him. He always encourages kids, as well as adults. By doing this, he makes people feel special. Most people like him because he is so nice to others. It has been sort of like dominos···when you are nice to other people they are nice back." An 8th grade student.

"The thing is, every kid has the potential to be a leader. You just have to get some of them out of their shell." Pete Kaligis, former Real Hero Mentor Role Model and University of Wyoming football coach.

The Puzzlewise Program

Several years ago I also founded an educational materials publishing company for grades 1 - 8 in the subject areas of math, science, language arts, and physical education/health. My company developed workbook materials that helped students learn the required grade-level learning objectives in a fun and exciting way. These educational materials inspired students to want to learn, and student learning quickly accelerated. This program also supported independent learning, allowing teachers to be more effective with increased flexible time.

I received many comments from satisfied principals, teachers, parents, and students; here are a few of them:

- "I am writing this letter as a thank you for your science resource. Our school has enjoyed great success on state standardized tests. In science this past spring our school had the most students either meeting or exceeding standard in the state (92.4%). Our science score is

actually in the top five percent of all schools at all levels in the state. The results were immediate; we realized a 22% increase in our state test scores within the first two years of adopting your program. Over the past four years we have scored in the top 10 percent or higher in the area of science. Teachers have found that using your materials during class time has helped them further individualize lessons to meet the specific needs of each student."
Dan S., principal.

- "The vocabulary program is stupendous! Even I've benefitted by working the program with my daughter!" Suzie C., home school mom of a 4th grader.

- "My class loves them. I even have 7th and 8th grade books and we work on them in groups. Thanks!" Erick A., 6th grade teacher.

- "I have only high praise for this program. The students are actually competing to see who can work the puzzles first. I have observed this in the classrooms." Kathy S., principal.

- "I come to class early so I can work on the next lesson. They're fun!" Wendy T., 5th grade student.

This just goes to show that there are materials available, and more being developed all the time, that can personalize education, inspire children, accelerate learning, meet learning objectives and provide the necessary flexibility for teachers to become more effective at building healthy children.

Footnotes

1. RSA Animate, the Royal Society for the Encouragement of Arts, London, United Kingdom.

2. 60 Minutes, CBS News.

3. National Institute on Drug Abuse (NIH)
http://www.drugabuse.gov/related-topics/trends-statistics/
infographics/abuse-prescription-pain-medications-risks-
heroin-use

4. Campaign to End Obesity
http://www.obesitycampaign.org/obesity_facts.asp

5. http://hotair.com/archives/2015/12/21/obama-its-the-
medias-fault-that-people-are-worried-about-isis-you-know/

6. Washington Post, April 2015.

7. http://www.nerdwallet.com/blog/credit-card-data/
average-credit-card-debt-household/

8. https://www.nerdwallet.com/blog/credit-cards/cost-of-living
-debt-metros-states/

9. http://www.fool.com/investing/general/2015/01/18/the
-average-american-has-this-much-debt-how-do-you.aspx

10. http://www.divorcereform.org/soc.html
[Whitehead, B. and Popenoe, D. The State of Our Unions.
Retrieved July 13, 2004 from http://marriage.rutgers.edu/
publications.]

11. Public Broadcasting System (PBS)
http://www.pbs.org/wnet/tavissmiley/tsr/education-under
-arrest/school-to-prison-pipeline-fact-sheet/

12. http://www.teenhelp.com/teen-pregnancy/teen
-pregnancy-statistics.html

13. http://www.cdc.gov/teenpregnancy/about/index.htm
National Campaign to Prevent Teen and Unplanned
Pregnancy, Counting It Up: The Public Costs of Teen
Childbearing 2013. Accessed May 21, 2014.

14. http://kff.org/other/state-indicator/overweightobese
-children/

15. http://jasonfoundation.com/prp/facts/youth-suicide
-statistics/

16. https://rainn.org/statistics

17. http://people.howstuffworks.com/public-schools1.htm

18. https://www.raceforward.org/research/reports/
historical-timeline-public-education-us

19. https://www.raceforward.org/research/reports/
historical-timeline-public-education-us

20. https://usergeneratededucation.wordpress.com/tag/
education-youth/   A Brief History of Education in the Freedom
to Learn series published in Psychology Today.

21. http://www.freedomworks.org/content/brief-history
-public-education-school-choice-america-part-ii

22. https://www.psychologytoday.com/blog/
freedom-learn/200808/brief-history-education

23. https://www.psychologytoday.com/blog/
freedom-learn/200808/brief-history-education

24. http://www.edweek.org/tm/articles/2015/10/30/why-the
-factory-model-of-schools-persists.html

25. NCCP | Child Poverty - National Center for Children in
Poverty
www.nccp.org/.../childpoverty.html

26. Why the Rich Live Paycheck to Paycheck - Betterment
www.betterment.com

Reality Quotes

"The purpose of life is not to be happy — but to matter, to be productive, to be useful, to have it make some difference that you have lived at all." Leo Rosten

"Live simply that others might simply live." Elizabeth Ann Seton

"Unless someone like you cares a whole awful lot, nothing is going to get better. It's not." Dr. Seuss

"It seems to me that any full grown, mature adult would have a desire to be responsible, to help where he can in a world that needs so very much, that threatens us so very much."
Norman Lear

"You are not here merely to make a living. You are here in order to enable the world to live more amply, with greater vision, with a finer spirit of hope and achievement. You are here to enrich the world, and you impoverish yourself if you forget the errand."
Woodrow Wilson

A Hundred Years From Now

A hundred years from now

it will not matter

what my bank account was,

the sort of house I lived in,

or the kind of car I drove...

but the world

may be different

because I was important

in making the world

a better place for ALL children,

those who are present now

and for ALL the generations to come.

Anonymous

About For Passion Publishing Company

FOR-PASSION
PUBLISHING

For Passion Publishing Company serves authors with an important message to share so everyone can enjoy the feeling of accomplishment and fulfillment. Many people want to write a book···have a great story to tell···a great truth to reveal···yet so few do. For Passion Publishing will make your dream come true so others can make their dreams come true, too.

For more information:

www.ForPassionPublishing.com